THE CERTIFICATION SERIES

Start Powerboating Right!

The national standard for quality on-the-water instruction

Published by the UNITED STATES SAILING ASSOCIATION   Copyright © 2011 by the UNITED STATES SAILING ASSOCIATION
ISBN 978-09821676-70.   Printed in the United States of America
UNITED STATES SAILING ASSOCIATION, P.O. Box 1260, 15 Maritime Drive, Portsmouth, RI 02871-0907

Introduction

Experience the Fun!

There is a sense of freedom and adventure when you're on the water – the freedom to explore, the freedom to spend quality time with family and friends, to go fishing, tubing, waterskiing, wake boarding, to connect with nature, and the freedom to get away to your own private paradise. This is part of what makes boating fun.

Courtesy of U.S. Coast Guard

The other part is a feeling of pride when you can handle your boat in challenging situations with no fuss or thunder and you look amazing in front of family and friends. When you as the skipper have the confidence and skills, your calm leadership sets the tone for everyone to relax and have fun.

For nearly three decades the United States Sailing Association and its US POWERBOATING have been conducting on-the-water courses, establishing standards for on-the-water instruction, and certifying instructors to teach on-the-water. They are considered the leading on-the-water experts for sail and power. In their Safe Powerboat Handling course, a person with no previous experience can progress rapidly from the introductory "dockside control" and docking drills to gain the confidence to perform high speed turns and stops. This is also a great course for those who want to improve their boat handling skills or recognize the need for continuing education.

There is a national network of waterfront boating centers, schools, marinas and clubs offering hands-on, on-the-water courses for sport and cruising powerboats using US POWERBOATING's standards and certified instructors. Try one of these courses and grab the power to experience the fun and adventure. For more information on these courses and participating waterfront facilities, go to *www.uspowerboating.com*.

Courtesy of Boston Whaler

Contents

1. The Powerboat

KEY CONCEPTS
▶ Types of boats   ▶ How a prop & jet work
▶ Parts of a boat   ▶ Engine controls

If it had been possible to come up with the perfect powerboat design, all powerboats would look nearly alike. However, there is an infinite variety of types and sizes aimed at fulfilling different boating activities.

Displacement Boats

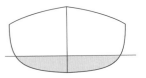

Displacement hulls create a bow wave as they push through the water. When the hull is trapped between a wave at the bow and another at the stern, it has reached its maximum speed.

Generally, boats with displacement hulls move "through" the water at slow to moderate speeds rather than riding on top of the water. This motion creates waves at the *bow* (front end), along the sides and at the *stern* (back end). As speed increases, the waves become larger and the distance between them lengthen until the hull becomes trapped between a wave at its bow and another one at its stern. When this happens, the displacement hull has reached what is called *hull speed*. This is the maximum speed for this hull. One of the most familiar examples of a displacement hull at hull speed is a tugboat moving at maximum speed with its hull sunk low in the water with a large bow and stern wave. Characteristics of displacement hulls include:

• Good maneuverability
• Good ability to hold a straight course
  (*directional stability*)
• Good load carrying capacity
• Good rough water handling
• Performance not greatly affected by load
• Speed limited by length (hull speed)
• May roll excessively when seas are
  coming sideways to the hull.

Planing Boats

A planing hull is designed to ride on top of the water once it has reached sufficient speed.

A planing hull behaves like a displacement hull at low speeds, forming waves at its *bow* (front end) and along the length of the hull. Upon reaching a certain speed it goes through a transition

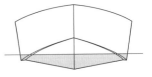

stage (*semi-displacement*) where it climbs the face of its bow wave. At this point the boat may become unstable, fuel consumption is high, and the operator may not be able to see over the raised bow. As the boat continues to accelerate it climbs on top of the bow wave and its bow levels off and the boat starts to plane along the top of the water with less wave making and using less fuel. But as the boat increases its speed past this point, wind and water friction on the hull also increase, causing a significant increase in fuel consumption. For most planing hulls the optimum fuel consumption with respect to distance traveled is achieved just as the boat has come comfortably on a plane. When a planing boat encounters waves, its ride can often become uncomfortable and at times even dangerously unstable. It may have to be slowed back to the displacement mode where it doesn't operate as well as its displacement cousin. There are several different shapes that can be used on a planing hull: flat, Vee and cathedral.

Flat-Bottom Hulls. Many planing hulls are variations of the flat-bottom hull. Flat-bottom characteristics include:
- Good load carrying
- Inexpensive to construct
- Below average in holding a course at low speeds — tend to slide or drift
- Rough riding in waves

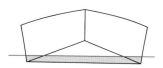

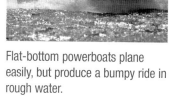

Flat-bottom powerboats plane easily, but produce a bumpy ride in rough water.

Vee-Bottom Hulls. The Vee-shaped hull, although a flat-bottom hull, has a pronounced Vee-shape to its bow where it cuts the water. Characteristics of this shape include:
- Good ability to hold a steered direction at speed
- Deeper Vees perform better in rough water
- Deep Vees tend to roll at rest

Vee-bottom powerboats have an angled bottom which improves ride and control in waves.

Cathedral Hulls. Cathedral hulls have two or three Vee shapes forward which turn into basically a flat hull aft. This gives greatly improved stability but with some of the unpleasant rough water ride as the pure flat bottom. Cathedral characteristics include:
- Good tracking at low speeds
- Good resistance to rolling even at rest
- Good load carrying capacity
- Tend toward lower *freeboard* (height of sides about the water)
- Uncomfortable at speed in rough water

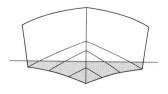

Cathedral hulls combine excellent stability and load carrying ability but produce a bumpy ride in waves.

Soft-Inflatable Hulls. These inflatables tend to be flat bottomed with the same rough and wet ride experienced in the pure flat-bottomed boat, perhaps even a little wetter. Their ability to hold a straight course is notoriously poor, particularly with any wind. The plastic impregnated fabric is susceptible to

Soft inflatables are popular for their light weight and convenient storage, but can be difficult to steer and are vulnerable to puncture.

the sun's ultraviolet radiation and can be sliced by sharp objects and chafed when dragging the hull up a rough beach or rubbing against a dock. In spite of these shortcomings they continue to be very popular due to their light weight, excellent buoyancy and stability at rest. Characteristics include:
• Light weight and portable
• High stability
• Very high buoyancy
• High load carrying capacity
• Soft contact with other boats but vulnerable to damage
• Easily affected by wind
• Low ability to hold a straight course (sideslips or drifts)
• Rough, wet ride at speed
• Relatively short life

A rigid-inflatable boat (RIB) combines the advantages of an inflatable with the control and seakindliness of a rigid Vee-bottom hull.

Rigid-Inflatable Boats (RIB's). These boats combine many of the advantages of the Vee-hull with the soft-inflatable. They have a rigid Vee-bottom (usually fiberglass) combined with the side buoyancy chambers of an inflatable. They have good performance in rough conditions, good directional stability along with the buoyancy and initial stability of the inflatable. They are heavier than the soft-hull inflatable and do not fold and store as conveniently.

Characteristics include:
• Combined advantages of Vee-hull with inflatable
• Good ability to hold a straight course
• High buoyancy
• Exceptional performance in rough water
• High load carrying capacity
• Soft contact with other boats
• Not as vulnerable to damage on bottom of hull as soft inflatable

Multihulls

A catamaran's narrow hulls and wide beam provide excellent stability and a smooth ride.

A catamaran with its two hulls connected by a platform has excellent stability. If each hull has an engine and propeller, a catamaran will turn easily. If it has only one engine and propeller between the hulls, it will be difficult to maneuver. Characteristics include:
• Good ability to hold a course at speed
• Good resistance to rolling
• Minimum *wake* (waves)
• Relatively shallow draft
• Cut through water rather than plane
• Small turning radius with two propellers
• Large turning radius with only one propeller
• Limited boathandling in bad weather

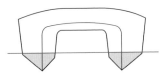

Personal Watercraft (PWC)

Personal Watercraft are frequently known by their common trade names, such as Jet Ski, Sea-Doo and WaveRunner. They use a water jet drive powered by a two-stroke or four-stroke gasoline inboard engine and are operated by a driver sitting on a saddle, or standing or kneeling. Characteristics include:
• Good agility and speed
• Good maneuverability except when rapidly reducing speed
• Driver may easily re-board after falling off
• No propeller or rudder to injure a person in the water

A handle bar is used to turn the nozzle of a water jet for steering a PWC.

Propulsion: Prop or Jet?

Propulsion systems generally consist of two major components: an engine that produces power and a drive unit that propels the boat. There are two essential types of powerboat drive units:
• a propeller (prop)
• a water jet (jet drive)

How a Propeller Works

A rotating propeller produces thrust that moves the boat. When an engine is in forward gear, the thrust from the rotating propeller drives the boat forward. When the gear is shifted into reverse, the propeller turns in the opposite direction driving the boat backward. Because propeller blades are optimized for forward thrust, their performance in reverse is drastically reduced.

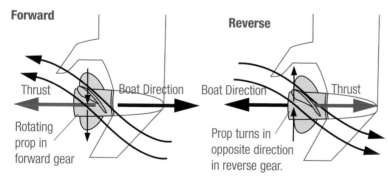

Thrust generated from a rotating propeller drives a boat forward.

A propeller rotating in the opposite direction drives a boat backward.

When viewed from behind, if a propeller drives a boat forward by rotating in a clockwise direction, it is defined as a right-hand propeller. If it rotated in a counterclockwise direction in forward gear, it would be left-handed. Whether a propeller is right- or left-handed will become important when "prop walk" is discussed in Chapter 5.

Propeller Rotation in Forward Gear

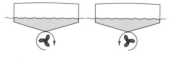

Right-Hand Propeller   Left-Hand Propeller

Contra-rotating propellers have two propellers, one in front of the other that rotate in opposite directions. This arrangement eliminates the wasteful twisting water flow from a single propeller as well as the prop walk (torque) effect. Advantages are increases in propeller efficiency, boathandling control, and fuel savings.

Propeller size is defined by its *diameter* and *pitch*, and these factors have an important effect on the performance of a boat. Pitch is the distance that a propeller would move forward in a solid material in one full rotation. For example, a propeller with a 17-inch pitch would advance 17 inches. Since water is a fluid, the propeller would actually travel a distance less than 17 inches. Larger diameter propellers with less pitch that rotate at lower rpm (revolutions per minute) are used for slow-speed boats or towing vessels, while smaller propellers with higher pitch operating at higher rpm are used for high-speed boats. A wrong propeller size may result in an engine overheating and/or a boat not reaching its designed speed.

Propeller Diameter

Propeller Pitch

High-Pitch Propeller

Low-Pitch Propeller

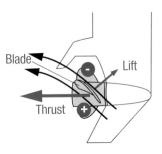

As a propeller rotates through the water, the pressure on one side of the blades is higher ⊕ than the other ⊖, which generates lift and thrust.

Water flowing over the surfaces of a propeller blade produces a higher pressure on one side than the other. This pressure difference generates *lift* which results in thrust as well as a sideways force (torque). If pressure on the low-pressure side of the blades gets too low, bubbles of vaporized water (low temperature steam) will form on the blades. This bubbling action disrupts the water flow, causing the blades to lose lift and thrust and the engine to speed up. This phenomenon is called *cavitation*. When it

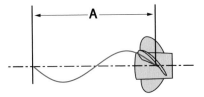

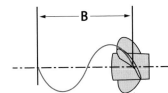

A low-pitch propeller (B) moves forward a smaller distance than a high-pitch propeller (A). The higher the pitch number, the greater the pitch (distance traveled per revolution).

occurs, reduce throttle and allow the propeller to "re-grip" the water. Cavitation can happen if too much throttle is applied too quickly, or if the propeller is damaged or not the right size, or plastic debris or kelp is wrapped around the propeller.

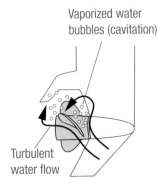

Cavitation causes the blades to lose lift and thrust.

How a Water Jet Works

A water jet has no propeller. Instead, water enters through an intake underneath the boat and is fed into a pump, which then accelerates it through a nozzle that produces thrust to move the boat.

Forward

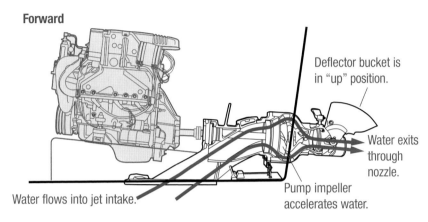

Deflector bucket is in "up" position.

Water exits through nozzle.

Pump impeller accelerates water.

Water flows into jet intake.

The jet of water exiting from the nozzle generates thrust to drive the boat forward. The nozzle can be pivoted sideways to turn the boat left or right.

Reverse

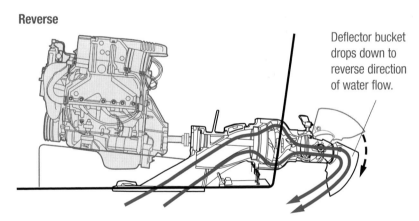

Deflector bucket drops down to reverse direction of water flow.

The deflector bucket reverses the jet of water to drive the boat backward.

Trim and Tilt Control

On stern drives and many outboard motors (typically above 25 hp) and jet drives, the angle of the drive unit to the boat can be changed (trimmed) while the boat is underway to achieve better performance. This is usually done by hydraulic rams, which are activated by a toggle button normally located on the throttle control lever. These hydraulic rams can also be used to tilt the drive out of the water when leaving the boat in the water or hauling out for storage or trailering. When operating in the trim range, the drive unit will move slowly, but once beyond the maximum UP trim position, the hydraulic speed will suddenly increase until the drive reaches its maximum tilt position. For more information on trim and how it affects a powerboat, see Chapter 5.

How a Dual-Function Control Lever Works

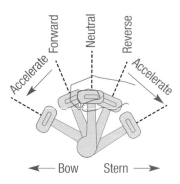

Side Mounted Dual-Function Control

Trim/tilt button

Neutral release lever - push into handle to move lever out of neutral.

Throttle only button - push in when lever is in neutral position to increase throttle while in neutral.

Engine Controls

Dual-Function Control. This is the most common type and has a single lever that combines throttle (speed) and gearshift (forward, neutral and reverse). It usually has a device that can disengage the gearshift to allow you to increase the throttle when starting or warming up the engine. Another feature of most controls is not allowing the engine to be started unless the gearshift is in neutral. If nothing happens when the ignition key is turned on, check to make sure the lever is in the neutral position. When shifting from forward to reverse or reverse to forward, pause briefly in neutral and count 1-2-3 to avoid damaging the gears.

Single-Function Controls. Another type of control has separate single-function levers, one for the throttle and the other for the gearshift, and can often be identified by the red (throttle) and black (gearshift) knobs on the levers. This type is sometimes used on larger boats with twin screws.

Using a Throttle Control. Changes in the throttle control should be done in a smooth gradual manner. When operating in conditions where the boat could impact waves or wakes, steady your hand on the base of the control and adjust the throttle with thumb and fingers.

Joystick Controls. These controls may be used on boats with fully rotating drive pods, jet drives or stern drives. Using a joystick is simple and intuitive. Move the joystick in the direction you want the boat to move; and twist the stick to rotate the boat around its pivot point.

Top Mounted Dual-Function Control

Here is a top mounted control with a single lever that controls throttle and gearshift.

Steady your throttle hand against the base in conditions where wake or waves are present.

Push the joystick in the direction you want the boat to go, or twist it to rotate the boat.

Parts of a Boat

The directions toward the ends of a boat are called *forward* (toward the front end) and *aft* (toward the back). The forward end is the *bow* and the back end is the *stern*. The *port* side of a boat is the left side and the *starboard* side is the right side when looking forward. Later on in the Navigation Rules chapter you will learn that the sidelights, which are turned on for nighttime operation, are a red color on the port side and green color on the starboard side.

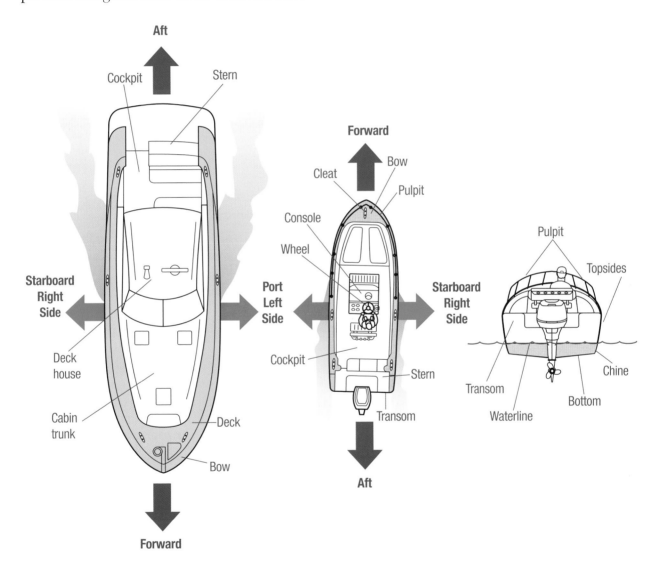

Boat Dimensions

The size of a boat is described by these dimensions.

Length Overall is used to determine the minimum safety equipment required for a boat by federal and state regulations. It is measured from the forward end to the back end of a hull. It does not include any parts attached to the hull, such as outboard motors, anchor rollers or swim platforms.

Beam is the maximum width of a boat.

Draft is the maximum depth below the water.

Freeboard is the height of the sides above the water.

Waterline Length is the length of a boat measured where it floats in the water.

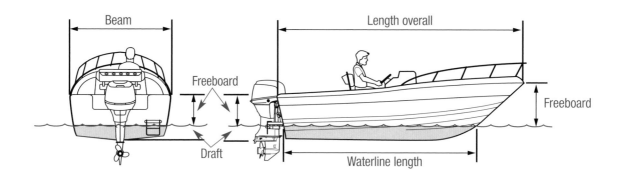

REVIEW QUESTIONS

1. The type of hull that moves "through" the water and has good rough water handling is a _____ hull. At higher speeds, it is the _____ hull that rises on top of the water, but may be uncomfortable in _____ water.

2. The optimum fuel consumption (best miles per gallon) for a boat on a plane occurs when just _____ on a _____.

3. Of the planing hull types, it is the _____ and _____ that have good performance in rough water.

4. When a planing hull begins climbing its bow wave, it is in the _____ stage. At this point the boat may become _____ , fuel consumption is high, and _____ may be poor over the raised bow.

5. Propeller size is defined by its _____ and _____.

Answers: 1) displacement; planing; rough 2) comfortably; plane 3) Vee-bottom; rigid inflatable 4) transition/ semi-displacement; unstable; visibility 5) diameter; pitch

2. Outboard Motors

KEY CONCEPTS
▶ Two- & four-strokes
▶ Outboard motor parts
▶ Starting procedure
▶ Fueling & maintenance

Two-Stroke & Four-Stroke

Outboard motors can range in size from small two-horsepower (hp) units that weigh 25 pounds to massive 300 horsepower (hp) engines. They can be either *two-stroke* (two-cycle) or *four-stroke* (four-cycle). Two-stroke outboards use oil mixed into the gasoline to lubricate the engine. Each "compression" stroke of a piston is followed by a "power" stroke (see illustration to the right). As the power stroke comes to its end, a new mixture of gasoline/oil and air enters the cylinder and exhaust gases are forced out along with some of the new incoming mixture. These outboards have been regarded as serious polluters, but recent innovations, such as oil injection and the replacement of carburetors with fuel injection, have reduced pollution to a level almost comparable to the four-stroke models.

Four-stroke outboards are lubricated by oil in the crankcase, similar to an automobile engine. An "intake" stroke, which brings in a mixture of gasoline and air, precedes each "compression" stroke, which is followed by a "power" stroke. The "exhaust" stroke, which forces out the exhaust gases, completes the cycle and the next cycle starts again with the "intake" stroke (see illustration to right).

As concerns about air and water pollution have increased, manufacturers have developed cleaner-running outboards. Some states have stringent pollution requirements for reservoirs and inland waters that may affect the use of your boat.

Parts of an Outboard Motor

Choke. A choke reduces the air supply in the carburetor, which enriches (increases the proportion of fuel) the fuel-air mixture that enters the cylinder. This makes the mixture easier to ignite. A manual choke control is pulled out to reduce or close the air supply. Some outboards may have an automatic choke and no action is required.

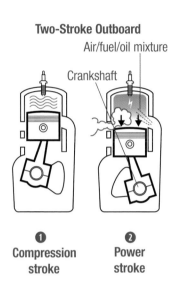

Two-Stroke Outboard

Air/fuel/oil mixture

Crankshaft

① Compression stroke

② Power stroke

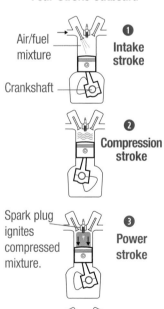

Four-Stroke Outboard

Air/fuel mixture

Crankshaft

① Intake stroke

② Compression stroke

Spark plug ignites compressed mixture.

③ Power stroke

④ Exhaust stroke

This symbol indicates a choke, which reduces air to the carburetor.

This primer pump knob ejects a small amount of fuel into the cylinder.

Primer pumps are used in many outboards. On electrically started engines, pushing in the key or just turning it to the "start" position activates a "primer" pump that injects a small amount of fuel into the cylinder. Manually activated primer pumps may be used on smaller outboards with manual pull-cord starting. At first glance these can be confused with a manual choke knob, but they are usually accompanied by a decal on the face of the engine listing instructions for use. Manual primer pump knobs must be pulled out and then pushed back in to inject the fuel. Some retract automatically while others must be pushed. If left out, the engine will not start.

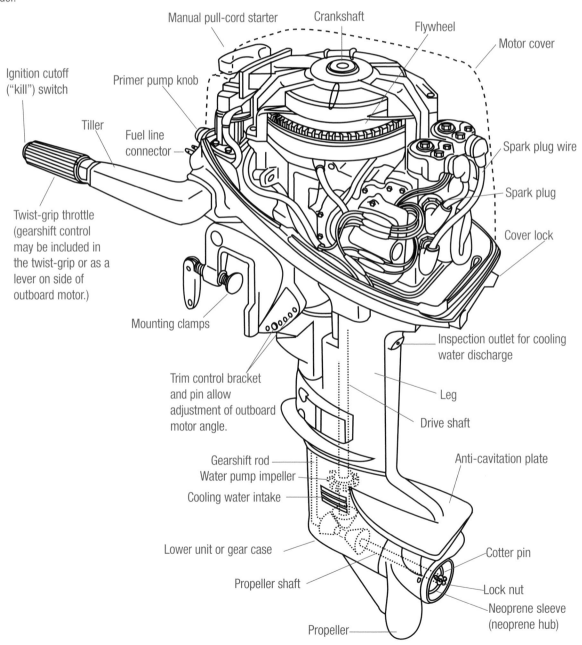

Two-Stroke Outboard Motor

Manual pull-cord starter

Crankshaft

Flywheel

Motor cover

Ignition cutoff ("kill") switch

Primer pump knob

Spark plug wire

Tiller

Fuel line connector

Spark plug

Cover lock

Twist-grip throttle (gearshift control may be included in the twist-grip or as a lever on side of outboard motor.)

Mounting clamps

Inspection outlet for cooling water discharge

Leg

Drive shaft

Trim control bracket and pin allow adjustment of outboard motor angle.

Gearshift rod

Water pump impeller

Cooling water intake

Anti-cavitation plate

Lower unit or gear case

Cotter pin

Lock nut

Propeller shaft

Neoprene sleeve (neoprene hub)

Propeller

Methods of choking or priming engines vary. Refer to the manufacturer's manual for starting procedures.

Tilt lock-release lever appears on small outboards without an electric-hydraulic powered trim /tilt control. The lever is in the "release" position when operating in forward gear, which allows the outboard to kick up if it hits an underwater object. It must be placed in the "lock" position before shifting into reverse to prevent the outboard from tilting up.

Twist-Grip Throttle and Gearshift. For outboards with a separate gearshift lever on the side of the motor, the twist grip throttle will usually have a shift position marked on it to which the throttle should be set before shifting the lever into forward, neutral or reverse so as to prevent serious damage to the outboard.

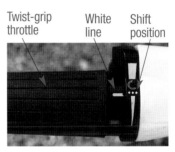

The white line on the twist-grip throttle is lined up with the shift position which will allow the gear to be shifted into forward, neutral, or reverse.

Four-Stroke Outboard Motor

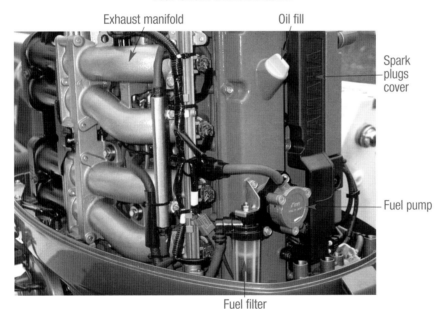

Exhaust manifold Oil fill Spark plugs cover Fuel pump Fuel filter

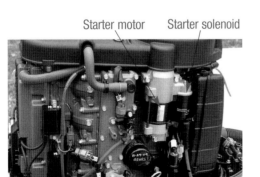

Starter motor Starter solenoid Oil filter Oil dipstick

Oil fill Spark plug Fuel pump Spark plug

Shear Pins and Safety Sleeves. All outboards have a designed weak link between the propeller and the propeller shaft to protect the engine and drive train if the propeller hits an object. Most outboards use a neoprene sleeve (neoprene hub) that is bonded to the propeller hub. When impact occurs, the bonding is broken, which protects the outboard. If the bond fails, there is usually enough friction in the neoprene hub to allow the engine to turn the propeller very slowly, often enough to return to safety. The propeller must then be removed and repaired. Smaller outboards may use a soft metal pin called a shear pin, which will break upon impact. Once the pin is sheared the propeller will no longer turn and it must be removed to replace the shear pin.

Outboard Inspection
- Outboard controls operate smoothly.
- Propeller blades, neoprene sleeve or shear pin are intact.
- Cooling water intake is clear.
- Oil level (applies to four-stroke or two-stroke with separate oil tank); add oil if indicated.
- Fuel tank level; add if indicated.
- Condition of fuel line (no cracks or sponginess) and connections.
- Any leaks in fuel system or gasoline odor in bilges.
- Condition of battery cables (no cracks, abrasion or frayed wire) and battery (no corrosion at terminals and proper fluid level). Cables securely fastened to battery.
- Condition of safety lanyard with one end securely connected to the ignition cutoff ("kill") switch.
- Attachment of safety chain, wire or line to boat and motor (applies to outboards fastened to the transom with screw clamps).

Outboard Starting Procedure

For best results, follow the procedures described in manufacturer's manual.
1. Complete the inspection.
2. Turn battery switch to correct setting.
3. Lower outboard into down position.
4. Pump the fuel primer bulb until it is firm (if using a portable or integral tank, open its air vent before pumping the bulb). Also pump oil bulb, if applicable.
5. Attach one end of the safety lanyard to the driver and make sure the other end is attached to the ignition cutoff ("kill") switch at the key ignition or on the tiller.
6. Center outboard motor.
7. Put gearshift in neutral and throttle to start position.

A *shear pin* breaks when a propeller hits an object, protecting the engine and the drive train from damage.

Most modern outboards use a *neoprene sleeve* bonded to the propeller hub that breaks when a propeller hits an object.

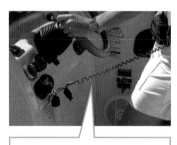

A *safety lanyard* attaches the driver to the ignition cutoff ("kill") switch. If the driver falls overboard or is thrown from the steering station, the engine will immediately shut off. Wireless cutoff devices are also available.

Photo Courtesy of U.S. Coast Guard

❽ If starting manually, activate the primer pump or pull the choke out all the way, then pull the starter cord until the engine starts. When using the cord remove any slack in it before pulling; don't yank on it or let it snap back on the rewind. On an outboard with a choke, once the engine fires, push choke in all the way (unless it is very cold). If after the third pull on the starter rope, the engine hasn't started, push the choke in halfway and pull the rope again. When using an electric start, push the ignition key in at the START position to activate the primer pump or choke. When the engine starts, release the key from the start position. It may be necessary to cycle the pump two or three times before engine fires. NOTE: *if starting a warm engine, do not use primer pump or choke.*

❾ Adjust throttle to steady idle.

❿ Check for a stream of water flowing from the inspection outlet for cooling water discharge. Important: If there is no water, turn off the outboard motor immediately to prevent damage from overheating.

⓫ Check gauges, if applicable. NOTE: If engine won't start and there is a smell of gasoline, wait several minutes before attempting to start it again.

Lifting an Outboard. A small outboard motor of 10 horsepower or less can usually be lifted and attached to a boat without too much effort. Although this is best done on land, when doing it on the water, tie the boat so it won't move around during the transfer. Have someone pass the outboard to a person in the boat. As a precaution against accidentally losing the motor overboard during the transfer, tie a retrieval line to the motor and fasten it to the dock or boat.

Retrieval line connecting motor and boat prevents motor from sinking to bottom if you lose your grip.

Outboard Cooling System

Most outboard motors are water cooled. The illustration tracks the flow of cooling water which enters through the cooling water intake, and is pushed up the water feed tube by a water pump and then circulates through waterways in the engine block. The water then flows back down the leg where it mixes with the exhaust gases and exits through the propeller hub. During its journey through the engine, a bit of the cooling water is diverted through the inspection outlet for cooling water discharge to let you know that the cooling system is working. Outboards smaller than five horsepower will usually have their exhaust outlet located just above the propeller instead of through the propeller hub.

Outboard Cooling System

Water circulates through the engine's waterways.

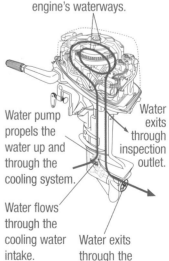

Water pump propels the water up and through the cooling system.

Water exits through inspection outlet.

Water flows through the cooling water intake.

Water exits through the propeller hub.

Fueling

Outboard Fuel System

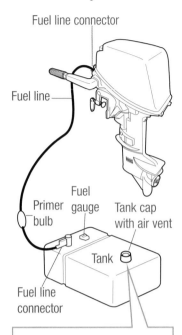

Fuel line connector

Fuel line

Primer bulb

Fuel gauge

Tank cap with air vent

Tank

Fuel line connector

Air vent must be open for fuel to flow to the outboard motor. It is usually closed when the boat is not being used.

Add gasoline fuel through the deck plate marked "gas" or "fuel" and carefully monitor the fuel flow.

Procedure for Two-Stroke Outboards. Oil is mixed with the fuel to lubricate the engine and there are two ways this can be done. To determine which method applies to your outboard, check the manufacturer's manual.

❶ *Adding oil to the fuel tank.* This method is most common in older engines. Oil is usually added first followed by gasoline to mix the ingredients. If the fuel tank is empty, add a gallon of gasoline before adding the oil, then add the rest of the fuel. Many outboards use a ratio of 1 pint of oil to 6 gallons of gasoline, but check the manufacturer's manual for the recommended ratio. Serious damage to the engine can result by using an improper mixture.

❷ *Adding oil to the oil tank.* Many newer two-stroke outboards have oil tanks (either as part of the engine or separately) that automatically meter the oil into the gasoline according to the engine speed.

Procedure for Four-Stroke Outboards. These run on gasoline with the lubricating oil added separately to the crankcase.

No matter what type of outboards is used, it is very important that you use the type of oil recommended in the manufacturer's manual.

Safety Precautions for Fueling. Always remember that gasoline vapor is heavier than air. It can settle in bilges or enclosed compartments and a spark can ignite an explosion. If the fuel tanks are portable:

• Fill them off the boat on the ground or the dock.
• Make sure the tank vents are open.
• Secure fuel fill caps and close the air vents before bringing them back on board the boat to avoid spillage.

If the fuel tank is built into the boat:

• Tie the boat to the dock to prevent it from moving and spilling gasoline during fueling.
• Close all hatches and openings before fueling.
• Shut off engine and all electrical equipment.
• Passengers should be off the boat.
• Do not overfill or force gasoline through the air vents.
• Close caps on fuel fills after fueling.
• Turn on blowers (if applicable) and open all hatches and openings and allow the boat to ventilate for at least four minutes.
• Check for gasoline odor in bilges and compartments before starting.

Use these precautions for fueling any kind of tank:
• Don't smoke or use anything that might cause a spark during fueling, such as matches, lighters or switches.
• Determine amount of fuel needed, but do not use a metal dipstick that could cause a spark.
• Keep the hose nozzle in contact with the tank or fill pipe to prevent a buildup of static electricity which might cause a spark.
• Leave some space in the tank for thermal expansion of the fuel.
• Allow time for fuel to drain from the hose before removing the nozzle from the tank.
• Wipe up spillage immediately and deposit rag in appropriate container ashore. Follow with a wash down if spillage was on the boat.

Maintenance

Outboards should be kept in good operating condition by regular inspection and maintenance and serviced periodically by a qualified mechanic. A tool kit with spare parts and manufacturer's manuals should be kept on the boat in a waterproof container.

Basic Tools and Spares
• pliers
• spark plug wrench
• screwdrivers (various types)
• knife
• sandpaper
• duct tape

• electrical tape
• spare shear pins (if applicable)
• cotter pins
• spare starter rope (if applicable)
• spare spark plugs

REVIEW QUESTIONS

1. Two-stroke outboards are lubricated by oil that is _____ into the fuel while four-stroke engines are lubricated by oil in the _____.

2. When starting a cold outboard, either a primer pump is used to inject a small amount of _____ into the _____ or a choke is used to reduce the _____ supply in the _____.

3. When a propeller hits an object, the rest of the outboard is protected from damage by breaking the bonding of the_____ to the propeller hub or breaking the _____.

4. When starting an outboard, it is important to check for a stream of _____ from the inspection outlet. If there is no _____ , the outboard motor should be _____.

5. After filling a built-in fuel tank, hatches should be opened to allow the boat to ventilate because gasoline vapor is _____ than air and can settle in the bilge.

Answers: 1) mixed; crankcase 2) fuel; cylinder; air; carburetor 3) neoprene sleeve/hub; shear pin 4) water; water; turned off 5) heavier

3. Inboard Engine Systems

KEY CONCEPTS
▶ Types of engines   ▶ Types of drives
▶ Starting procedures   ▶ Fueling & maintenance

Inboard engines use either gasoline or diesel fuel. Gasoline engines with their relatively lighter weights and higher rpm often power high-performance sportboats. Diesel engines are typically used on large or moderate-speed vessels for their reliability and low-speed torque. Diesel fuel does not have the fire hazards of gasoline.

Gasoline Engine Systems

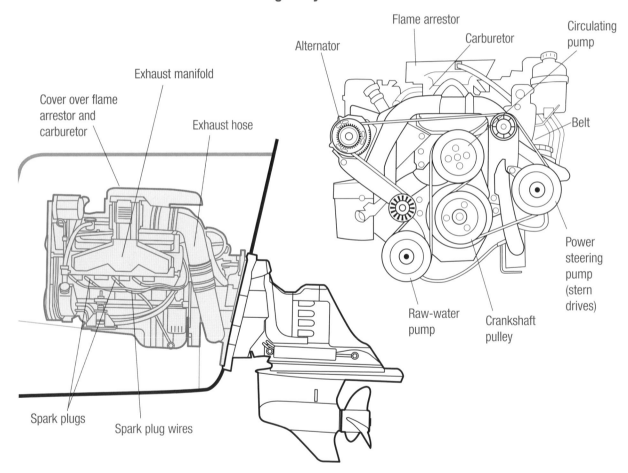

Gasoline Engine Inspection
• Oil level; add if indicated.
• Fuel tank level; add if indicated.
• Condition of fuel line (no cracks or sponginess) and connections.
• Any leaks in fuel system or gasoline odor in bilges.
• Belts should be snug; look for signs of wear.

- Raw-water *seacock* (valve) should be open.
- Raw-water strainer; clean out debris.
- Engine control levers operating smoothly.

Gasoline Starting Procedure. Follow procedures in the manufacturer's manual for recommended steps.

❶ Complete the inspection.

❷ Turn battery switch to correct setting.

❸ Engage engine blower for at least four minutes or until all traces of gasoline odor have disappeared.

❹ Tilt stern drive into down position and center it (if applicable).

❺ Put gearshift in neutral (throttle slightly open if necessary).

❻ Turn ignition key to ON to start engine.

❼ Adjust throttle to steady idle.

❽ Check gauges (oil pressure, water temperature, ammeter).

❾ Check exhaust outlet for consistent water flow.

Diesel Engine Systems

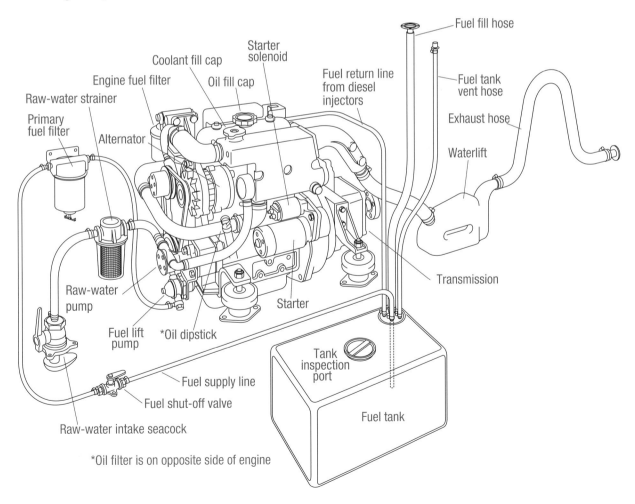

*Oil filter is on opposite side of engine

Diesel Engine Inspection
- Engine oil level; add if indicated.
- Coolant; add if indicated.
- Fuel tank level; add if indicated.
- Condition of fuel line (no cracks or sponginess) and connections.
- Belts should be snug; look for signs of wear.
- Engine pan and bilge for fuel, water or oil.
- Raw-water *seacock* (valve) is open.
- Raw-water strainer; clean out debris.
- Engine control levers for smooth operation.

Diesel Starting Procedure. Follow procedures in the manufacturer's manual for recommended steps.
1. Complete the inspection.
2. Turn battery switch to correct setting.
3. Put engine control in RUN position.
4. Put gearshift in neutral (throttle slightly open if necessary).
5. Preheat with glow-plug control for 10-30 seconds, if applicable.
6. Turn on ignition (oil pressure alarm should sound) and start engine.
7. Adjust throttle to steady idle (oil pressure alarm should stop).
8. Check gauges (oil pressure, water temperature, ammeter).
9. Check exhaust outlet for consistent water flow.

All diesel engines are stopped by depriving the engine of fuel. This is achieved by either using a mechanical pull or by an electro-mechanical device using a button or a different key position. CAUTION: *Do not stop engine when in forward or reverse gear.*

Cooling Systems

Nearly all inboard engines use seawater (raw-water) to cool the internal coolant, unlike a car which uses air to cool the internal coolant.

Types of Drives

Stern Drives. Stern drives, sometimes called inboard/outboards (I/O) or outdrives, combine features of both an inboard engine and outboard motor. The gasoline or diesel engine is mounted inside the boat and the power train goes through the transom to a stern drive that resembles the lower part of an outboard motor. The stern drive is turned to steer the boat and is also capable of being tilted upward when not in use.

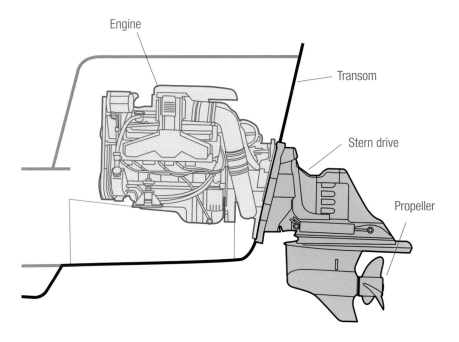

Shown is a typical stern drive driven by an inboard engine.

Stern Drive Inspection

• Hydraulic fluid for power trim control (reservoir generally mounted on inside of transom); add if indicated.

• Propeller blades and neoprene sleeve are intact.

Shaft Drives with "Fixed" (Non-Swiveling) Propellers. The propeller shaft starts at the gearbox transmission and passes through a sealed stern tube in the bottom of the hull. Since the propeller cannot be turned like an outboard motor or stern drive, a rudder is required to steer the boat.

Shown is a typical shaft drive with a fixed propeller driven by an inboard engine.

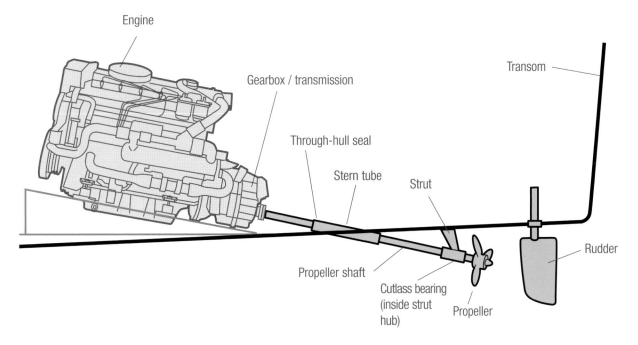

Stuffing Box Seal

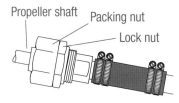

"Dripless" or "Packless" Seal

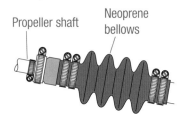

Propeller Shaft Through-Hull Seal. There are various arrangements for sealing the shaft as it passes through the hull. The most common is the "dripless" or "packless" seal which uses carbon or PTFE (Teflon). Another type is a stuffing box packed with flax rings which is designed to leak a small amount of water, a few drops per minute, when the shaft is turning to help keep it lubricated. A packing nut on the stuffing box is tightened against the packing material to keep the water flow to a few drops per minute.

Jet Drives. Jet drives use a large water pump impeller powered by either a gasoline or diesel engine to accelerate water flow through a nozzle to produce propulsive thrust. Jet drives have good steering ability at all speeds except when slowing down. Most mid- to large-size jet drives use deflectors for steering and reverse by deflecting the water flow from the nozzle to change direction. Smaller jet drives used on personal watercraft (PWC) and small sportboats may use a swiveling nozzle for steering and a reversing deflector.

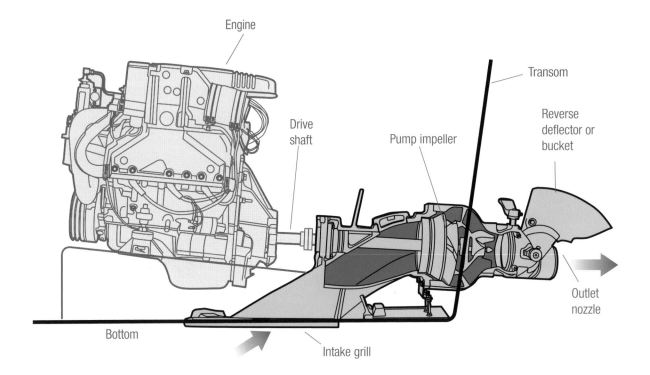

Jet Drive Inspection
- Jet drive control should operate smoothly.
- Hydraulic oil level; add if indicated.
- Condition of jet drive's impeller; inspect through access cover (engine must be turned off and transmission in neutral).
- Jet drive should rotate freely (engine must be turned off and transmission in neutral).

Pod Drives. These increase maneuverability, especially during close-quarters maneuvers, and improve performance and fuel efficiency. They are generally installed as twin pods on powerboats with a mid-30 foot length and larger. The pods can be rotated for directional thrust and are typically controlled with a joystick which also can be twisted to pivot the boat within its length. A pod drive system includes a:

• Propeller drive unit with contra-rotating propellers either rear-facing (e.g., Mercury Zeus, ZF Marine) or forward-facing (e.g., Volvo IPS) on the pod
• Transmission control unit (inside the hull)
• Engine (diesel or gasoline)

Fueling

Gasoline Engines. Use gasoline fuel with lubricating oil added to the engine through the oil fill opening. Remember that gasoline vapor is heavier than air and can settle in bilges or enclosed compartments. All it takes is a spark to ignite the vapor and cause an explosion. Safety precautions for fueling:

• Close all hatches and openings before fueling.
• Passengers should be off the boat.
• Shut off engine and all electrical equipment.
• Do not smoke or use anything that might cause a spark during fueling, such as matches, lighters or switches.
• Determine amount of fuel needed and do not overfill or force gasoline through the air vents. Allow room in the tank for thermal expansion.
• Keep the hose nozzle in contact with the fill pipe to discharge the buildup of static electricity from the fuel to prevent a spark.
• Allow time for fuel to drain from the hose before removing the nozzle from the tank.
• Close caps on fuel fills after fueling.
• Turn on blowers and open all hatches and openings and allow the boat to ventilate for at least four minutes or until all traces of gasoline odor have disappeared.
• Wipe up spillage immediately and deposit rag in appropriate container ashore. Follow up with a wash down if spillage occurs on the boat.

Diesel Engines. These run on diesel fuel with lubricating oil added separately through the oil fill opening. Although diesel fuel is much less volatile than gasoline and is considered relatively risk-free when fueling, it is still good practice to follow many of the safety precautions for gasoline fueling.

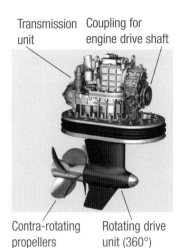

Transmission unit Coupling for engine drive shaft

Contra-rotating propellers Rotating drive unit (360°)

Make sure fuel is added only through the deck plate marked "diesel" or "fuel" and monitor fuel flow continuously to avoid overfill.

Maintenance

Consult the manufacturer's manual for recommended maintenance procedures. A basic tool kit with spare parts for repairs and maintenance as well as manufacturers' manuals should be kept on board the boat in a waterproof container.

Basic Tools and Spares
- pliers (include water pump pliers)
- wrenches (include stuffing box wrench if applicable)
- spark plug wrench (if applicable)
- screwdrivers (various sizes and heads)
- hammer
- knife
- sandpaper
- duct tape
- electrical tape
- spare spark plugs (if applicable)

REVIEW QUESTIONS

1. Inboard engines use either _____ or _____ fuel. _____ fuel does not have the fire hazards of _____.
2. Before starting a gasoline engine, the engine blower must be turned on for at least _____ minutes.
3. After starting an inboard engine, it is important to check for _____ flowing out of the exhaust outlet. If there is no _____, immediately _____ the engine.
4. A diesel engine is normally stopped by
    a. turning off electricity to the engine
    b. engaging the brake on the shaft
    c. depriving the engine of fuel
    d. depriving the engine of air
5. Jet drives have good steering ability at all speeds except when _____.

Answers: 1) gasoline; diesel; Diesel; gasoline 2) four 3) water; water; turn off 4) c. depriving the engine of fuel 5) slowing down

4. Preparation & Operator Responsibilities

KEY CONCEPTS
▶ Preparation & trip planning
▶ Equipment & departure checks
▶ Crew briefing
▶ Life jacket wear
▶ Operator responsibilities
▶ Knots & line handling

Preparation and planning are without question the most important ingredients in safe, enjoyable powerboating. Many of the things that can go wrong can be avoided with a bit of foresight.

Wearing Life Jackets

Wearing life jackets is comparable to wearing seat belts in a car. If you're wearing one, it could save your life if you fall overboard or your boat gets swamped with water. Boating conditions can change rapidly and it is especially important to wear a life jacket in severe weather, cold air or water conditions, unsafe conditions such as rough inlets, high boat traffic at night, and if you're alone or in remote areas. Trying to put a life jacket on while in the water can be difficult and tiring. Your life jacket should:
• be an appropriate size
• fit properly so it doesn't ride up when you are in the water
• be a visible color when in the water (yellow or orange are the most visible)

If your boat is registered anywhere in the U.S., life jackets must be U.S. Coast Guard approved. For more information on the five types of approved life jackets, see Chapter 10.

Dress for Boating

Nothing takes the fun out of boating faster than being cold — or hot. Temperatures on the water tend to be more extreme and more changeable than ashore, so the right gear and clothing are an important part of enjoying your time on the water. Using the layered approach to clothing is the best way to stay comfortable in changing conditions. In cool weather, it's important to keep your head, hands and feet warm.

Because damaging ultraviolet (UV) rays can penetrate clouds and bounce off the water's surface, it's important to protect your eyes and skin. Apply sunscreen with a Sun Protection Factor (SPF) of 15 or higher that protects against both UVA and UVB rays. This will provide

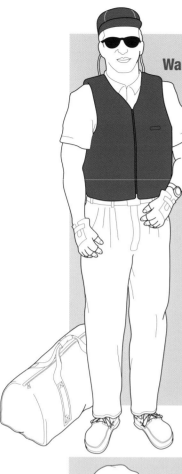

Warm Weather Dressing

- Light-colored hat or visor with a dark color under the bill to reduce reflection.

- UV sunglasses with a keeper cord.

- Light-colored, lightweight cotton shirt. For sun-sensitive skin, a high collared shirt with sleeves helps protect neck and arms.

- Life jacket in good condition zipped or clipped closed.

- Water-resistant watch.

- Long pants protects legs from prolonged exposure to the sun.

- Snug-fitting shoes with non-skid soles for firm traction on wet surfaces and foot protection.

- Soft, water-resistant duffel bag contains foul-weather gear, cold-weather or spare clothing, bathing suit, towel, sunscreen, and a water bottle.

Cold and Wet Weather Dressing

- A fleece or knit ski cap helps minimize heat loss through the head.

- Hood with brim and drawstring keeps head and neck dry and warm. A baseball cap worn under the hood provides the protection of a visor and keeps the hood out of your vision when turning your head.

- Fleece jacket with high collar with or without nylon shell. For colder conditions, add additional layers for warmth over synthetic (polypropylene, polyester) underwear.

- Life jacket worn outside foul-weather gear.

- Velcro or elastic cuffs at wrists and ankles help keep water out.

- Lined waterproof gloves keep hands dry and warm.

- Foul-weather gear offers protection from wind and water.

- For colder conditions, add a layer of fleece pants.

- Sea boots with wool or synthetic socks keep feet warm and dry.

protection from both direct and reflected sunlight. Waterproof and "SPORT" sunscreens are available which will not run or rub into eyes. Wear sunglasses with good protection from:
• Sideways exposure
• UV rays (at least 90%)
• Glare off the water (polarized lenses)

A two-piece foul-weather gear set with a waterproof jacket and pants (preferably with suspenders) is more versatile than a one-piece jumpsuit. The jacket and pants can be worn together or separately to suit different temperatures and conditions. When selecting a size, make sure it is loose enough for layers of warm clothing underneath.

Checking Weather

Develop a habit of checking local conditions and forecasts before departure and be conscious of weather developments while underway. Wind direction and speed are especially important because they can affect your route, the time of your departure and return, and even whether it is safe to make the trip. The NOAA weather radio network broadcasts local and coastal marine forecasts on a continuous cycle. Most VHF radios can receive these broadcasts, usually on a channel listed as WX1, WX2, etc. There are numerous Internet websites, including the National Weather Service (NWS), that provide local marine weather information as well as weather chart analysis and forecasts, radar images, and warnings. If you know the web address of your local NWS office, you can save time by going there directly. Weather applications that can be downloaded onto your mobile phone is another excellent resource for current conditions, forecasts, radar images, and severe weather warnings and advisories. Many television weather reports provide live radar coverage of your boating area. This is particularly valuable in determining the potential for thunderstorms. In any event, take time to get the best weather forecast available. (See Chapter 12 for more information about weather.)

ONLINE... National Weather Service local weather information: http://www.srh.noaa.gov/

Checking Tide and Current

When using a boat ramp or operating in tidal waters it is important to know the status of local tides to ensure there is enough water at the ramp or along your intended route. In many areas currents can have a major effect on navigation (particularly on slower boats) or using a ramp. Currents flowing perpendicular to ramps in rivers and tidal estuaries can often make *launching* and *hauling out* a challenge. In these situations it is important to know the times of slack water (minimal or no current) and maximum current flow. Remember, slack

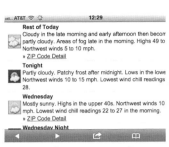

A weather forecast screen from a mobile phone.

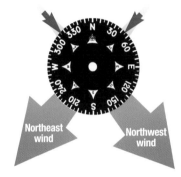

Wind direction is defined as the direction the wind is blowing from, not blowing to. A wind blowing from the Northwest to the Southeast is called a Northwest (NW) wind. Direction may also be defined by the compass direction in degrees, such as 315 degrees. You can also determine the wind direction using visual or sensory indicators: flags, smoke or trees on land, wind ripples on the water, or the feel of the wind on your face or neck.

Tide Definition:
Tide is the vertical rise and fall of the water level due to gravitational pull of the moon and sun.

Current Definition:
Current is the horizontal movement of water caused by tides, wind, the flow of rivers, or ocean streams. Its direction is defined as the direction the current is flowing toward.

An example of tide information which can be downloaded onto your mobile phone.

Current is flowing past this anchored buoy.

NAVLOG **RC TO FYC**

From	To	Crs	Dist	Speed	ETE	ETA	Remarks
RC	MK "E"	087	.5	5	0+06	0+06	
MK "E"	FG 7	048	2.3	6	0+23	0+29	
FG 7	FG 5	352	1.9	6	0+19	0+48	
FG 5	FYC	272	1.6	5.5	0+30	1+18	Slow at 1+00

This sample navigation plan depicts compass courses, distances, speeds and times for various marks along the route.

water does not always coincide with high and low tide. Sources for tidal and current information include nautical almanacs, tidal current tables, NOAA weather radio broadcasts, applications that can be downloaded onto your mobile phone, newspapers and television. (See Chapter 12 for more information about tides and currents.)

Local Hazards

It is also important to know of any special or out-of-the-ordinary situations that might affect you. These may include missing or changes in navigation marks, bridge closures, diving operations and dredging. A good source for this information is the U.S. Coast Guard's *Local Notice to Mariners*, which is updated weekly and available for download from its Navigation Center. You can also sign up to receive free automatic notices by email. The U.S. Coast Guard also broadcasts marine safety information and notices to mariners twice a day on Marine VHF Channel 22A. Special notices such as missing navigation marks are also broadcast as they occur in safety broadcasts on Channel 16 in Urgent Marine Broadcasts.

ONLINE... U.S.C.G Navigation Center: http://www.navcen.uscg.gov/
Local Notice to Mariners (LNM): http://www.navcen.uscg.gov/?pageName=lnmMain
Sign up for LNM: http://www.navcen.uscg.gov/?pageName=LNMlistRegistration

Take local weather hazards into account when planning a boating trip. These can include strong onshore sea breezes that occur as the land heats up during the day, squalls, thunderstorms, lightning and fog. (See Chapter 12 for more information.)

Navigation Plan

A Navigation Plan should be created in advance of your departure. Although every trip on familiar waters does not require a detailed navigation plan, there should be some method to find your way home. A laminated page showing compass headings from a conspicuous, lighted, sound-buoy (a navigation aid) to your destination can be invaluable in limited visibility. Unfamiliar waters demand a more detailed plan of compass headings, distances and estimated times that can be backed up with GPS positions of latitude and longitude.

Float Plan

Someone else should know your plan — where you plan to go, your route plan and departure and arrival times as well as a complete description of your boat, names of people on board, type of radio and boat name, and survival gear carried on board. Write this information down either on a sheet of paper or a prepared form. This is called a

Sample Float Plan

Complete this form before going boating and leave it with a reliable person who can notify the Coast Guard or other rescue organization, should you not return as scheduled. Do not file this plan with the Coast Guard.

1. Person Reporting Overdue

Name _____ Phone _____

Address _____

2. Description of Boat

Registration/Documentation No. _____

Length _____ Make/Year _____ Type _____

Hull Color _____ Trim Color _____ Fuel Capacity _____

Engine _____ No. of Engines_____

Distinguishing Features _____

3. Operator of Boat

Name _____ Age _____ Gender _____

Phone _____ Medical Conditions_____

_____

Address _____

Operator's Experience _____

4. Survival Equipment (Check as Appropriate)

No. of Life Jackets _____ No. of Flares _____ Mirror _____ Smoke Signals _____

Flashlight _____ Food _____ Paddles _____ Fresh Water _____

Anchor _____ Raft or Dinghy _____ EPIRB _____

Others _____

5. Marine Radio

☐ Yes, ☐ No Type _____ DSC MMSI No. _____

6. Trip Expectations

Depart from_____ Departure Date_____ Time_____

Going to_____ Arrival Date_____ Time _____

If operator has not arrived/returned by: Date _____ Time _____ call the Coast Guard or local authority at the

following number: _____

7. Vehicle Description

License No. _____ Make _____ Model _____ Color _____

Where is vehicle parked?_____

8. Persons on Board

Name _____ Age _____ Gender _____

Phone _____ Medical Conditions_____

_____

9. Remarks _____

_____

Float Plan. Give it to a friend or relative (not the Coast Guard) who can contact the Coast Guard if you don't return on schedule. Writing the information down is important. Not only is it difficult for someone to recall these details from memory, but the very process of writing it down forces you to think about your trip and plan more thoroughly. Upon your return, let your friend or relative know that you have arrived safely.

Boarding

Your boat should be tied to the dock or slip to keep it from moving. Step aboard the boat where it's closest to the dock. If you're carrying something, place it in the boat first or have someone hand it to you after you're aboard. Use both hands to grab something solid on the boat. To get better balance when stepping onto a smaller boat, keep your body low by bending over or squatting. On small, light boats, try to step as closely as possible to the centerline to minimize tipping. Once you are in a boat, your weight may affect how the boat sits in the water. Position your weight so that the boat is level from side to side and neither the bow and stern are too far down.

Departure Checks

A simple laminated list can be an invaluable aid in assuring that nothing has been overlooked. Some of the items on your list should include:

- Prepare appropriate foods and liquids.
- Check current weather conditions and forecasts.
- Determine tides and currents.
- Identify local hazards.
- Review relevant charts, updates and cruising guides.
- Prepare a Navigation Plan and estimate fuel requirements.
- Determine viable alternatives or ports of refuge.
- Prepare a Float Plan and leave it with someone.
- Check the required equipment is present, up to date and in good working order.
- Complete the engine inspection checks (see Chapter 2 for outboard motor inspection and Chapter 3 for inspection checks of inboard gasoline and diesel engines).
- Remove water that has accumulated in bottom of the boat.
- Add fuel for trip.
- Complete crew briefing.
- Complete the pre-start list.

Operator Responsibilities

An operator is responsible for the safety of the boat and everyone on board as well as others affected by his or her actions. To operate a boat responsibly and safely you should follow these guidelines:

- Do not exceed the Maximum Capacities plate or label. This is required for all powerboats (except inflatables) smaller than 20 feet in length built after October 31, 1972 and must be permanently displayed and visible to the operator. If the boat has no Maximum Capacities marking, a rough guide is to multiply the length by the beam in feet and divide by 15 to get a maximum number of people. Exceeding weight or horsepower limits could result in capsizing or swamping.
- Reduce the risk of falling overboard by briefing everyone to sit in seats while underway, not on seatbacks, or on the bow, side decks or transom; and if they have to move around to keep a secure grip on the boat.
- Avoid sudden changes in speed and direction that could cause your passengers to lose their balance or fall overboard. If you have to make a sudden change, give a timely warning.
- Always maintain a proper lookout for other vessels, hazards, swimmers and divers.
- Always operate your boat at a safe speed and observe speed limits.
- Know your boat's performance capabilities and limitations.
- Monitor fuel to make sure you have enough to return with an adequate reserve.
- Follow your navigation plan and keep track of your position.
- Be alert for any weather changes and listen periodically for weather updates on the weather channel of your VHF radio.
- Know the Navigation Rules and use them to avoid collisions (see Chapter 13). If an incident results from your neglect to comply with the Navigation Rules or take seamanlike precautions, there is nothing in the Rules that will release you from this important responsibility. You are expected to be aware of dangerous situations and a departure from the Rules may be necessary to avoid immediate danger.
- Avoid impeding the passage of tug and barge traffic and large vessels that can only navigate within a channel.
- Be considerate of others. Minimize the effect of your boat's wake, especially near docks or paddle craft liable to capsizing in waves. Remember, you are responsible for any damage caused by your wake.
- Be aware of the hazards of a propeller to people in the water. Position the boat to keep the propeller away from anyone in the water, or preferably turn off your engine until they are clear.
- Avoid disturbing the natural habitat of wildlife. In some areas, large animals such as manatees in Florida share the waters and you should use caution to avoid them.

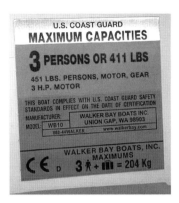

Maximum Capacities Label or Plate is required on powerboats with a length of less than 20 feet, except for inflatable boats.

For boats with outboard motors the label must display:
- Maximum number of persons and weight (persons weight is controlling)
- Maximum weight capacity including persons, engine and gear
- Maximum horsepower of the engine

Boats with inboard engines the label must display:
- Maximum number of persons and weight (persons weight is controlling)
- Maximum weight capacity including persons and gear

Crew Briefing

Briefing people once they are on board the boat is an important safety measure. Boat operators too often assume their passengers have more experience than they actually have and are competent swimmers with no medical problems. Be aware of any health issues and the swimming ability of your passengers in case these become an issue if they fall overboard or the boat swamps. The briefing should include the following:

- Discuss the importance of keeping hands and feet inside the boat.
- Identify the "safe" (cockpit) and "danger" (side decks, riding on the bow) areas on a boat.
- Point out location of fire extinguishers, life jackets, flares, first aid kit, and bilge pumps.
- Explain what to do with garbage, and how to operate the boat's marine toilet.
- Indicate what is expected of them when leaving or returning to a dock or slip and while the boat is underway or anchoring.
- Describe some basic emergency procedures, such as how to use the radio in an emergency or turn off the engine, and what they should do if a person falls overboard or if dangerous weather conditions occur.

Types of Line

There are several different types of line (rope) used on boats:

- Nylon is commonly used for anchor lines (rodes) and docklines because of its strength and ability to stretch, which helps absorb shock loads.
- Polyester or Dacron line has less stretch and less ultimate strength than nylon, but is easy on the hands. It is a good all-purpose line.
- Polypropylene line is not as strong as Nylon or polyester line and is very sensitive to UV radiation, but it floats, which makes it popular for waterskiing towlines. It has a slippery surface and doesn't bend easily, so be careful when tying knots in polypropylene line.

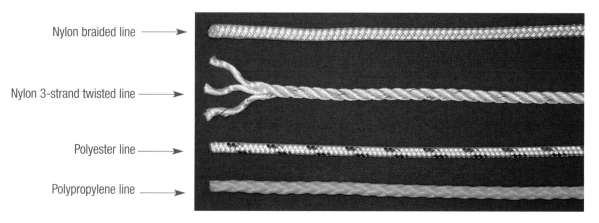

Nylon braided line
Nylon 3-strand twisted line
Polyester line
Polypropylene line

Knots

Safe powerboating requires basic seamanship functions such as tying up to a dock, using fenders, securing an anchor line, taking a tow and giving another boat a tow. All of these cases involve handling a line (rope) and tying a secure knot that is also easy to untie.

ONLINE... Knot tying videos (knot tying techniques may vary slightly):

http://uspowerboating.com

http://www.animatedknots.com/indexboating.php?LogoImage=LogoGrog.jpg&Website=www.animatedknots.com.

Cleat Hitch. A cleat hitch is used to tie a line to a cleat. If tied properly, the line won't jam or slip on the cleat.

Round Turn with Two Half-Hitches. This knot can be used to secure fender lines to rails or stanchions.

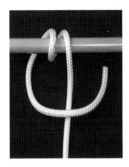

Wrap the end of the line *twice* around the object.

Cross the end over and around the standing part, passing it inside to form a half-hitch.

Again, cross the end over and around the standing part, passing it inside to form a second half-hitch.

Bowline. This knot can be used to make a non-slipping loop at the end of a line to put over a piling or cleat. It becomes more secure under pressure, but remains easy to untie when pressure is released. In situations where the load on the line is not constant, it can work loose. For that reason, it is not recommended for tying an anchor line to an anchor.

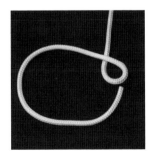

Make a small loop near the end of the line. Make sure the end crosses on top of the standing part of the line.

Pass the end up through the loop, down behind the standing part, back up over the edge of the loop, and down through the loop.

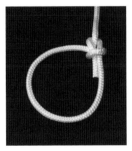

Tighten the knot, making sure the knot holds and the remaining loop does not slip.

Cleat Hitch

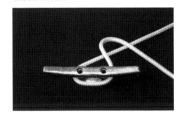

Lead the line around the far end of the cleat and wrap it around the base.

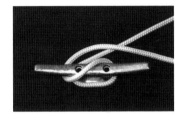

Cross the line over the top and around the horn.

Then twist the line to form a loop around the other horn.

The end of the line should parallel the part of the line that was originally crossed over the top of the cleat.

Sheet Bend

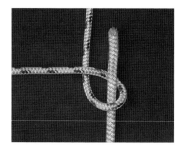

Make a loop at the end of the smaller line with the bitter end crossing over on top. Run the larger line up through the loop.

Run the larger line under and around the standing part of the smaller line, and back through the loop again.

Tighten the knot.

Shows the sheet bend from the other side.

Sheet Bend. A sheet bend is used to tie the ends of two lines together and is properly tied if the two ends are on the same side of the knot. If the ends are on opposite sides, the knot tends to slip. The sheet bend holds well with lines of different sizes, but is most secure if the lines are the same size.

Handling Docklines with End Loops

Normal practice when approaching a dock is to give the person on the dock the end of the line with the loop in it and then direct him where to place the line. The line is then adjusted from the boat.

Using a Loop on a Cleat. If a loop is simply slipped over a cleat, changes in tension and angle of the line could cause the loop to jump off the cleat. Taking a turn around the cleat with the loop reduces this possibility. Another method is to pass the loop through the opening of the cleat before putting it over the ends (horns) of the cleat. A loop on a cleat cannot be freed if it is under load.

Pass the loop through the opening in the cleat. Then pass the end of the loop over the horns and tighten the line.

Taking a turn around a cleat with the loop reduces the possibility of the loop jumping off accidentally.

Dipping a Loop. If a line is to be placed around the piling and another boater has his loop already around the piling, your loop should be passed up through the other boat's loop before being placed over the top of the piling. This allows either boat to leave without removing the other loop.

Larger line

The loop of the larger line has been dipped under and inside the smaller line's loop before passing it over the piling.

Making a Larger Loop. If the loop on a line is too small to fit around the piling, the line can be passed through the loop to make a larger one.

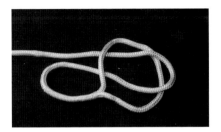

Grab the line about 18 inches below the loop and pass it through the loop.

Then pull on the line. The part of the line closest to the loop will pass completely through, forming a larger loop.

Coiling a Line

When you have finished using a line, it should not be simply left in a tangled pile. Idle lines should always be coiled so they are ready to use or release.

When coiling a line, one hand makes a new loop that is fed onto the other hand holding the loops previously coiled.

- *Twisted* line (three strands twisted into a rope) is sensitive to whether it is coiled in a clockwise or counterclockwise direction and should be coiled in round loops with no figure-8s. Most twisted lines are twisted in a right-handed direction and should be coiled in a clockwise direction, otherwise they will kink when uncoiling.
- *Braided* line does not have twisted strands and has no preferred coiling direction, but will typically coil into figure-8 loops. To ensure the coils will run freely with no kinks, the loops may need to be alternated in direction or coiled in figure-8s.

Stowing a Coiled Line. When a line is not being used or is stowed in a locker, it should be secured in such a way to prevent it from getting tangled.

When coiling twisted lines, it helps to twist or rotate the line slightly to make round loops with no figure-8s.

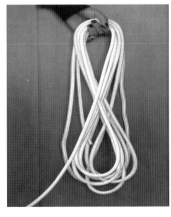

When coiling braided lines, they will have figure-8 loops which will run freely with no kinks.

Stowing a Coiled Line

Wrap the end of the line three times around the coil, then make a loop in the end and pass it through the upper hole.

Pass the loop over the coil and bring it down to the wraps.

Pull the end of the line to tighten and secure the coil.

Heaving a Line

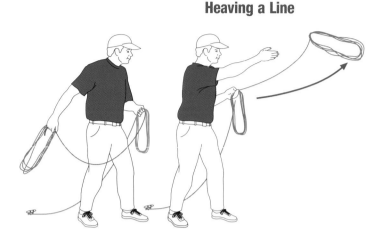

When preparing to throw a line, first make sure one end is secured on your boat. Hold half of the coil in your throwing hand and the other half in your other hand. Swing and throw the coil underhand, allowing the remainder of the line to run free from your other hand. Don't throw the line right at the person, but just to the side.

Securing a Boat

A powerboat can be tied alongside a dock with single bow and stern lines and two spring lines, which minimize the forward and after movement of the boat, or it can be positioned in the middle of a slip with two bow lines and two stern lines.

Line Handling Commands

Sometimes handling docklines may require precise instructions so that both the operator and the line handlers are on the same page and the lines are adjusted as needed. Here are some definitions of basic line handling commands.

CAST OFF – Untie and let go lines.
TAKE IN – Untie lines from shore and bring them on board.
SLACK – Take off all tension and let the line hang slack.
EASE – Let line out until tension is eased but line is not slack.
CHECK – Hold heavy tension but not enough to part the line.
HOLD – Do not let any line out but be ready for more maneuvering.
SURGE – Momentarily release tension on a line to let a stopped boat move.
MAKE FAST – Secure a line.

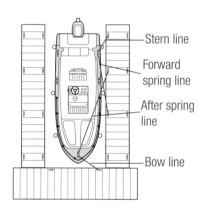

Stern line
Forward spring line
After spring line
Bow line

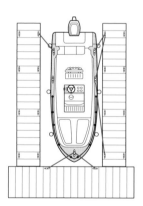

Each dockline has a specific name and just the basics will be covered here.
- A *bow line* is fastened to the bow of a boat and runs forward at about a 45 degree angle to the dock.
- A *stern line* is fastened to the stern of a boat and runs aft at about a 45 degree angle to the dock.
- *Spring lines* are named based on where they originate and the direction that they run from a boat. On small boats the point of origin is generally omitted from the name and this convention will be used in this book.
- An *after spring line* is fastened to either the bow or an amidships cleat (toward the center of a boat) and runs aft from the boat to the dock.
- A *forward spring line* is fastened at the stern or to an amidships cleat and runs forward from the boat to the dock.

REVIEW QUESTIONS

1. With regard to clothing, the best way to stay comfortable in changing weather conditions is to use the _____ approach.

2. Local weather conditions and forecasts can be found on the Internet and television in addition to _____ marine weather reports on VHF radio.

3. The Local Notice to Mariners is a good source for information on _____.
   a. navigation plans
   b. ship departures
   c. clothing advice
   d. local hazards

4. A Float Plan should not be given to the Coast Guard, but to a _____ or _____.

5. Due to its ability to stretch more than other types of line, the line generally preferred for anchor and docking lines is _____.
   a. Dacron
   b. nylon
   c. polypropylene

Answers: 1) layered 2) NOAA 3) d. local hazards 4) friend; relative 5) b. nylon

5. Boathandling Concepts

KEY CONCEPTS

▶ Putting a boat in motion
▶ Stopping
▶ Wheel & tiller steering
▶ Steering with directed thrust
▶ Steering with a rudder
▶ Prop walk

▶ Steering with twin screws
▶ Boat's pivot point
▶ Minimum control speed
▶ Holding position
▶ Balance & trim
▶ Use of spring line

Putting a Boat in Motion

Putting a boat in motion involves shifting into forward or reverse gear at a low throttle setting and then adjusting the throttle to achieve the desired speed. *The key concept to remember when shifting to forward, neutral or reverse is that it should be done at idle rpm* to prevent damage to the engine or transmission.

Stopping

Since a boat has no brakes, the throttle and gearshift controls are used to stop it. Reducing the throttle to idle speed and shifting into neutral will eliminate thrust from the propeller or jet, but the boat will still keep moving until its momentum is dissipated. The faster the boat is moving, the more time and distance it will take to lose momentum and come to a stop.

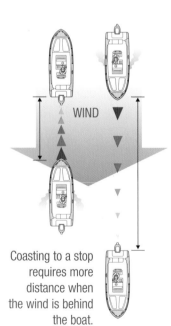

WIND

Coasting to a stop requires more distance when the wind is behind the boat.

Coasting Stop. Reduce the throttle gradually, then shift into neutral. You can stop without using reverse, but you need to allow distance for coasting to a stop. Less coasting distance is needed if you stop heading into the wind. Larger and heavier boats carry more momentum and coast farther than small boats. The larger the boat, the more distance it will coast.

Quick Stop. If a boat needs to be stopped more quickly in a shorter distance:
❶ Gradually reduce throttle to idle rpm.
❷ Shift into neutral and pause briefly (while counting 1-2-3).
❸ Shift into reverse and increase throttle slightly to overcome forward momentum and stop boat.
❹ Bring throttle to idle rpm and shift into neutral.

Using a Wheel or Tiller to Steer

On boats with wheel steering, turn the wheel in the direction you want to turn just as you would a car. For boats with tiller steering, move the tiller opposite to the direction you want to turn.

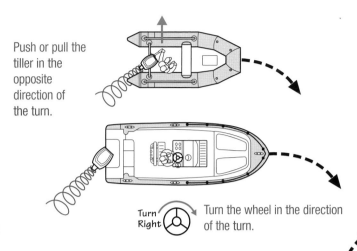

Push or pull the tiller in the opposite direction of the turn.

Turn Right

Turn the wheel in the direction of the turn.

Steering with Directed Thrust

All boats with outboard motors, stern drives and jet drives use the *directed thrust* of the propeller or jet to steer the boat. To generate directed thrust, the propeller has to be turning (in forward or reverse gear) or the jet drive has to be pumping water through it. If the engine or jet drive is in neutral, the boat cannot be steered.

When the outboard motor is turned, the directed thrust from the propeller swings the stern (back end) of the boat, causing the boat to turn. To make a tighter turn, turn the outboard all the way to the side and increase the amount of thrust by increasing the throttle.

Steering with a Rudder

Boats with a "fixed" propeller drive use a rudder to produce a sideways force to turn the boat. Water must be flowing past the rudder to create this steering force. This flow is produced by the boat's motion through the water and by the propeller. As a boat moves faster, the steering ability of the rudder improves because the side force it generates increases as the speed of the water flow increases. To increase the effectiveness of a rudder in forward motion, it is normally placed behind the propeller to take advantage of the additional flow of water generated by the propeller (called *prop wash*). At very slow forward speeds you can use a momentary pulse of prop wash by briefly increasing the throttle to increase the flow of water passing the rudder, which increases the turning force. This is a technique often used when maneuvering at slow speeds in a confined area.

An outboard uses directed thrust from its propeller to turn the boat.

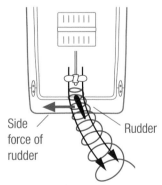

Side force of rudder

Rudder

A boat with a fixed propeller uses a rudder to turn the boat.

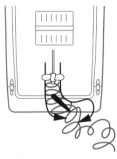

A rudder requires smooth water flow around it to function. Turning the rudder too sharply can stall flow and cause loss of steering.

Steering with Prop Walk (What is Prop Walk?)

Prop walk is a side force produced by the rotation of the propeller. This side force causes your boat to turn slightly rather than go in a straight line. Prop walk is most noticeable when the engine and propeller are operating in reverse on boats with a fixed propeller and rudder. A right-hand propeller in reverse "walks" the stern (back end) to port (left). A left-hand propeller in reverse will "walk" the stern to starboard (right). Increasing the throttle will increase the amount of prop walk, which will swing the stern even more.

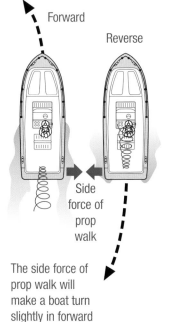

The side force of prop walk will make a boat turn slightly in forward and reverse.

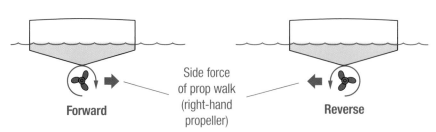

This tendency can be put to good use if you anticipate which way it will move your boat. You can test your prop walk direction by putting the boat in reverse while still tied to the dock. Center the wheel and compare the amount of water flow (wash) on both sides of the boat. The stern will move away from the side with the greatest flow when in reverse.

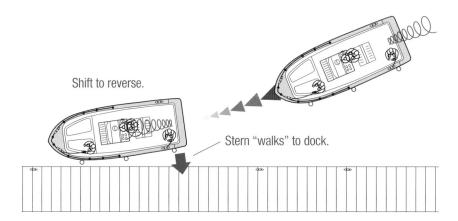

Prop walk can be used to advantage in docking when the propeller is operating in reverse gear. You will want to approach the dock along the side of your boat that "walks" toward the dock. As you reach the dock, reverse your engine and let the stern "walk" alongside.

Steering with Bow and Stern Thrusters

Bow thrusters have become standard equipment on many large powerboats and are becoming increasingly popular on more moderate sized boats. Thrusters are used to increase a boat's maneuverability by moving either the bow of the boat sideways with a bow thruster or the stern sideways with a stern thruster. Both types of thrusters typically use one or two propellers contained in a tunnel to generate sideways thrust. They are either electrically or hydraulically powered.

Steering with Twin Screws (Propellers)

Propellers on twin-screw powerboats typically rotate in opposite directions to counteract each other's side force (prop walk). If both throttles are set at the same rpm, the prop walk effect is negated and the boat will go forward and backward in a straight line.

A boat can use thrust from an individual propeller or a combination of both for turning. When the port (left) propeller turns in forward gear and the starboard (right) propeller is in neutral, thrust will turn the boat to starboard (right) in a wide turn. To make an even tighter turn, put one propeller in forward gear and the other in reverse. If one throttle is advanced more than the other, the corresponding propeller will create more thrust and prop walk, causing the boat to turn.

Thrust from the bow thruster rotates the bow away from the dock.

Typical rotation in forward gear

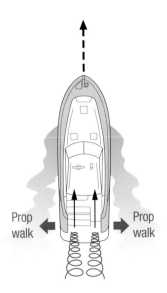

Prop walk ← → Prop walk

With throttles set at same rpm, the thrust and prop walk from each propeller is equal and opposite and the boat will run in a straight line.

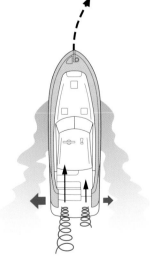

With one throttle set at higher rpm, that propeller produces more thrust and prop walk, causing the boat to turn.

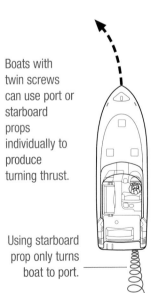

Boats with twin screws can use port or starboard props individually to produce turning thrust.

Using starboard prop only turns boat to port.

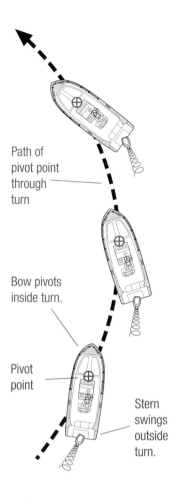

Path of pivot point through turn

Bow pivots inside turn.

Pivot point

Stern swings outside turn.

Pivot Point

A boat's pivot point is the point around which it appears to turn. This point is normally located from 25% to 40% aft from the bow. As the boat starts to move forward, the pivot point shifts slightly forward and then moves aft as speed increases. When a boat turns, the relationship of the turning thrust at the stern to the pivot point causes the bow to rotate toward the direction of the turn and the stern to swing away from it.

When the boat goes backward, the pivot point appears to move aft considerably, causing the bow to swing in a wider arc than the stern.

Many good drivers imagine they are steering just the pivot point. They visualize the path they wish their pivot point to take over the water and then steer the point along that path. When a boat makes a turn, the first part of the turn will be wider than the rest of the turn.

Turning Concepts

When making a turn, a key concept to remember is that a boat rotates around a pivot point, which causes the stern to swing out wide of your turning path. Keep this in mind when passing close to an object in the water. While your boat's bow and pivot point may clear the object, your stern could hit it.

At low speeds with reduced thrust from a propeller or jet, wind and current will have greater effect on steering control and turning maneuvers. In tight maneuvering situations, it may be necessary to use intermittent pulses of increased thrust by briefly advancing the throttle to improve turning control or make a tighter turn.

Wind Direction Clues
- *smoke from a smokestack*
- *flags onshore*
- *boats on moorings (usually point into the wind unless being affected by current)*
- *ripples or waves*
- *wind on your face (boat has to be stopped)*

Windage

Wind will have an important effect on almost all of your boathandling maneuvers, especially when you operate at lower speeds in moderate to strong wind conditions. The wind's impact varies with the amount of the boat's surface area (*windage*) that the wind pushes against. Boats with high topsides, cabins and flying bridges have greater windage than boats with lower profiles.

Boats have a tendency to turn away from the wind.

WIND

When drifting, the wind will usually cause the bow to "fall off" until the boat lies across the wind or even with the stern toward the wind. This tendency to turn away from the wind is an important consideration when holding a boat in position.

When turning into the wind, windage reduces your speed and tightens your turning arc. This can be beneficial when maneuvering in a confined area.

When turning with the wind, windage increases your speed and enlarges your turning arc.

Underwater Hull Shape

A boat's underwater hull shape will affect its steering characteristics. Boats with minimal underwater profile, such as soft inflatables, will tend to skid or sideslip along the surface of the water as they turn, thereby increasing the turning arc. Turning this type of boat in windy conditions in a confined area is a true boathandling challenge.

Minimum Control Speed

Minimum control speed is the slowest speed at which you can operate and still maintain steering control. Typically, this is less than the speed produced when the engine is in gear and the throttle is set at idle rpm, and is accomplished by the use of *intermittent power*. With the throttle at idle rpm, shift from neutral to forward and back to neutral. This produces a short, gentle pulse of power to maintain steering control. Repeat this technique to keep the boat under control and moving slowly. Minimum control speed is used in many situations such as docking and operating in confined areas. It is shown in the illustrations by ▶▶▶▶ .

To make turns at minimum control speed, position the wheel (*helm*) in the desired direction and shift into forward gear at idle rpm to start the turn, then back to neutral near the end of the turn. As a result of the directed thrust from the propeller (or increased water flow over the turned rudder), the boat will turn but not accelerate significantly. When using intermittent power to turn, avoid oversteering and using too much throttle to prevent loss of steering control.

Holding Position

There are times when you may have to hold your boat in a specific location such as helping a boat in trouble, waiting for a bridge to open or waiting for room at a dock. The key to holding position is to anticipate boat drift and make small, gentle corrections early rather than large powerful corrections late Always position the wheel (helm) in the direction you want to go before applying power.

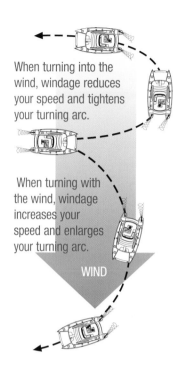

When turning into the wind, windage reduces your speed and tightens your turning arc.

When turning with the wind, windage increases your speed and enlarges your turning arc.

WIND

Minimum Control Speed Steering
When steering at minimum control speed, turn the helm to the desired direction while in neutral, then shift into gear.

Turn prop small amount and shift to forward to bring bow back into wind.

Turn Right

Holding Bow into Wind. Since the bow will usually have a tendency to turn away from the wind, you will have to compensate for this by periodically shifting into forward gear and making slight steering corrections to bring the bow back into the wind. Don't let the bow fall off (turn away from the wind) too much. When the bow is pointed into the wind, shift back to neutral and drift back to your holding position. If the boat drifts downwind of the position, shift into forward gear to bring it back in position. Repetitive small adjustments must be made to maintain a holding position, especially as the wind increases. When current has more influence than wind, hold position with the bow or stern into the current, not the wind.

Holding Stern into Wind. Because the bow wants to turn downwind, it is usually easier to hold position with the stern into the wind, provided waves don't come over the transom (back end). Shift into reverse to keep the stern headed into the wind and to compensate for drifting. In windy conditions, you may have to switch to holding the bow into the wind to avoid exposure to exhaust gases or taking water over the back of the boat.

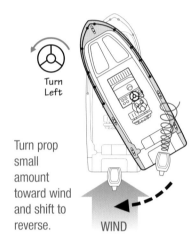

Turn Left

Turn prop small amount toward wind and shift to reverse.

WIND

Balance and Trim

Boat balance and trim affect not only boat speed and fuel consumption, but also steering. A boat that leans to one side will be out of balance and will tend to turn. To correct this problem, you can move passengers and gear to level the boat and lower the trim tab on the low side. If the condition is not corrected, it could result in loss of steering control and possibly capsize smaller boats.

Left side is lower.

This boat is not balanced from side to side and will turn.

A boat with too much bow-down or bow-up trim will lose speed and is less responsive to steering. Too much bow-down trim may also bring the propeller too close to the water surface, sucking air onto the blades, and causing it to lose thrust. When this happens there will be a sudden increase in engine rpm and a sudden slowing in the boat.

Outboard motor trimmed down produces bow-down trim.

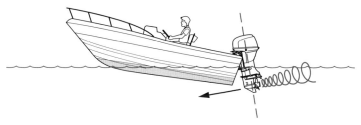

Outboard motor trimmed up produces bow-up trim.

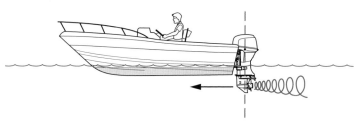

Outboard motor trimmed level to water surface produces level trim.

A boat's fore and aft trim can be controlled by adjusting the up/down trim angle of the propeller or by adjusting trim tabs. A hydraulic trim control is used on larger outboards to adjust propeller angle.

Speed Modes

When a planing boat is moving, it will be operating in one of three speed ranges or speed modes:

Displacement Speeds. The boat rides through the water at almost level trim and is easy to steer and maneuver. As it approaches the semi-displacement mode, the stern squats and the bow rises as the boat's bow wave increases in size.

Semi-Displacement Speeds. Most boats operate very inefficiently with high resistance at this speed. They have bow-high trim with the bow riding up the bow wave, producing maximum wave making (wake). They are sluggish to steer and maneuver. It requires a lot of power (throttle) to counteract the high resistance of the bow wave. In shallow waters, the stern will squat more, producing greater wake and the possibility of striking the bottom.

Adjusting Trim
An outboard motor or trim tabs trimmed down can get a boat on a plane more quickly. Once on a plane, the outboard or trim tabs should be trimmed up until the boat is at optimum speed and rpm. When encountering waves, trim down to lower the bow and allow the boat to drive through the waves.

Trim tabs are used to keep boat level and running straight.

In displacement mode, a boat glides smoothly in level trim with minimum wake.

In semi-displacement mode, the boat labors in bow-up trim. Maximum wake is produced.

In planing mode, boat rides level on top of water with less wake.

Planing Speeds. The boat rides on top of the water at close to level trim, supported by dynamic lift. Its wake has decreased in size, speed has increased significantly, and the boat responds quickly to small steering changes. Hydraulic trim controls can be adjusted to achieve optimum speed for a fixed throttle setting.

Changing Speeds

Increasing Speed. The speed modes help to explain how a boat's operating characteristics change as power is added or reduced. As a boat increases speed, the bow raises and maintaining visibility becomes a problem, especially close ahead. Collision accidents are often the result of one or both boats operating in this mode of restricted visibility. Before opening the throttle, always check to make sure your course is clear of hazards. Whenever increasing speed raises the bow, stand up if the boat has a standup steering station or console, and adjust the trim tabs and/or trim angle of the outboard or stern drive to lower the bow and maintain your close-ahead vision.

Reducing Speed. When slowing down from a planing speed to a displacement speed, the boat will transit through the semi-displacement range again, generating increased *wake* (waves).

Boat Wake

Be considerate about the wake produced by your boat. You are responsible for any damage or injury caused by your wake. Adjust your speed to reduce your wake when passing:
• boats tied to a dock or slip or rafted alongside each other
• boats in a mooring area or at anchor
• boats with people fishing
• a sailboat with a person aloft on the mast

Reduce wake by operating at slower displacement speeds (preferably) or planing speeds. Operating at planing speeds in an anchorage is unsafe because of higher collision risk with another boat operating at high speed that may be hidden from view behind a moored boat. Changing speed to reduce wake should be made well in advance since it takes at least several boat lengths for your wake to settle down.

Spring Lines

A spring line is a dockline that can work as a lever to turn a boat when you motor against it. It is used when leaving or returning to a dock and slip in adverse wind or current conditions.

Using an After Spring Line. Motor against it to rotate the stern away from a dock.

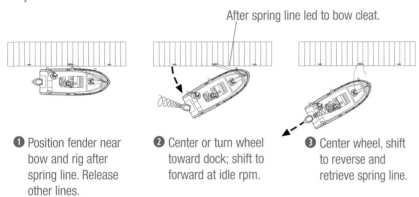

After spring line led to bow cleat.

❶ Position fender near bow and rig after spring line. Release other lines.

❷ Center or turn wheel toward dock; shift to forward at idle rpm.

❸ Center wheel, shift to reverse and retrieve spring line.

Using a Forward Spring Line. Motor against it to rotate the bow away from a dock.

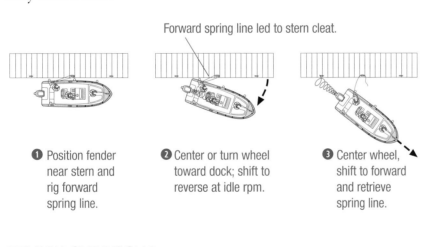

Forward spring line led to stern cleat.

❶ Position fender near stern and rig forward spring line.

❷ Center or turn wheel toward dock; shift to reverse at idle rpm.

❸ Center wheel, shift to forward and retrieve spring line.

REVIEW QUESTIONS

1. With the engine in neutral, outboard motors, stern drives and jet drives have _____ steering.
   a. poor b. good c. excellent
2. The sideways force generated by a propeller is called _____.
3. Steering a boat at minimum control speed requires _____ of power.
   a. no pulses b. gentle pulses c. strong pulses
4. A boat will produce maximum wake in the _____ mode.
5. A line running from a bow cleat to a cleat on the dock near the stern of a boat is called a/an _____ spring line and when you motor against it the boat's _____ will swing away from the dock.

Doubling a Line

Doubling a dockline allows you to release a line from aboard the boat without any assistance from a person on the dock.

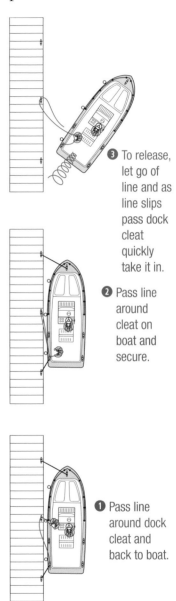

❸ To release, let go of line and as line slips pass dock cleat quickly take it in.

❷ Pass line around cleat on boat and secure.

❶ Pass line around dock cleat and back to boat.

Answers: 1) a. poor 2) prop walk 3) b. gentle pulses 4) semi-displacement 5) after; stern

6. Boathandling – Directed Thrust

KEY CONCEPTS
▶ Leaving & returning   ▶ Turning maneuvers

Leaving a Dock

Key Points
- *Make sure everyone understands what to do with docklines and fenders.*
- *Check that no lines (ropes) are in the water before starting the engine.*
- *Start the engine using the manufacturer's recommended procedure.*
- *Stow docklines and fenders once clear of the dock.*

Back-Away Departure. Backing away from a dock usually offers the best maneuvering control. It also avoids a problem inherent to forward departures when the boat starts to turn and its stern (back end) swings into the dock, preventing the boat from departing cleanly.

Departure Using Directed Thrust Steering
❶ Turn wheel away from dock, which rotates propeller away from dock. If using a tiller, move it toward dock.
❷ Shift into reverse, stern (back end) swings away from dock as boat backs away. To avoid scraping the bow (front end) against dock, keep your turn small until bow clears dock.
❸ When clear of dock, turn wheel or tiller in opposite direction to turn boat parallel to dock.
❹ Center wheel or tiller, pause briefly in neutral, then shift into forward.

During a forward departure from a dock, the stern can swing into the dock, preventing the boat from completing its turn.

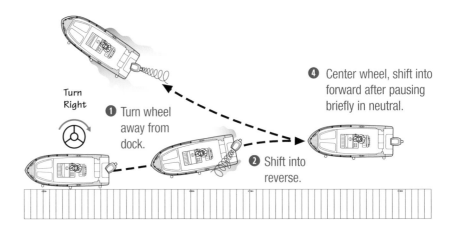

Turn Right
❶ Turn wheel away from dock.
❷ Shift into reverse.
❹ Center wheel, shift into forward after pausing briefly in neutral.

Straight-Ahead Departure. This method is often used when a boat is positioned near the end of a dock and can clear the dock with little, if any, turning. It can also be used if a crosswind or crosscurrent will make the boat drift clear of the dock. Remember that when turning, your stern (back end) will swing outside your intended track and could hit the dock.

❶ Center outboard, release docklines.
❷ Shift into forward gear and steer a straight course until clear of dock.
❸ Turn when clear of dock.

CAUTION: An injury could occur when using a hand or foot to push a boat away from a dock. If you have to push off, sit or stand in the cockpit and use a boat hook (pole).

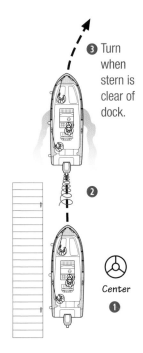

❸ Turn when stern is clear of dock.

❷

Center

❶

Leaving a Slip

Departure Using Directed Thrust Steering
❶ Center wheel (or tiller) and shift into reverse, slowly backing straight out.
❷ Turn boat once bow is clear of slip.
❸ Center wheel (or tiller) and shift into forward after pausing briefly in neutral.

Turning Maneuvers

Avoidance Turn. This maneuver is used to prevent the stern of your boat from swinging into an obstacle when you've turned too late or too close. The initial turn away from the object positions the boat's pivot point away from it, and the turn back pivots the stern away from the object and avoids a collision.

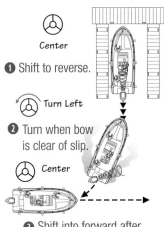

Center

❶ Shift to reverse.

Turn Left

❷ Turn when bow is clear of slip.

Center

❸ Shift into forward after pausing briefly in neutral.

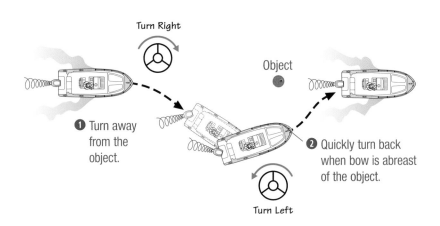

Turn Right

Object

❶ Turn away from the object.

❷ Quickly turn back when bow is abreast of the object.

Turn Left

Pivot Turn

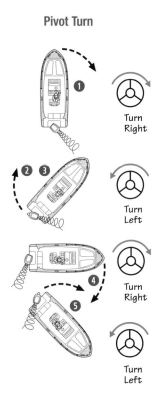

Backing Downwind

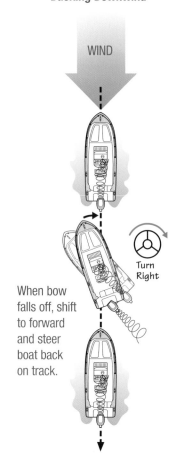

When bow falls off, shift to forward and steer boat back on track.

Pivot Turn Using Directed Thrust. This is a maneuver frequently used in marinas or other very confined spaces to rotate a boat within a space of one to two boat lengths.

❶ Starting at rest, turn wheel hard over to one side and shift into forward gear at idle rpm to initiate pivot turn.

❷ Shift into neutral and turn wheel hard over in opposite direction.

❸ Shift into reverse at idle rpm to continue turn.

❹ Shift into neutral and turn wheel hard over in opposite direction.

❺ Repeat until boat has completed its turn.

NOTE: To rotate the boat in the opposite direction, just reverse the direction of the wheel listed in steps ❶, ❷ and ❹.

Driving Backward

Key Points

• *Wind direction: the bow will tend to turn downwind.*

• *Sea conditions: backing smaller outboard boats into waves may result in water coming over the transom and flooding the well or cockpit. If this starts to happen, abandon this maneuver.*

• *The pivot point will move aft in reverse, and depending on the boat's underwater shape and windage, it may move essentially to the propeller. This is particularly true for outboards or stern drives.*

• *Steering control: when backing and turning in reverse, use small steering adjustments. Too large or too fast adjustments can lead to a loss of control.*

Backing Toward the Wind.
The combination of windage and pivot point will help you hold your course.

Backing Downwind. It may be more difficult to maintain your course when backing downwind. If the bow falls off too much, you will lose steering control. Before this happens, shift to forward gear and bring the boat back on course. Then back up again with perhaps a slight steering correction to compensate for the wind's effect.

When backing a boat, use small steering adjustments to keep it under control.

High-Speed Maneuvers

When running at higher speeds, a boat is less affected by wind. Other considerations become important, such as sea conditions, wake from other boats and semi-submerged objects in the water. Hard impact at high speed can cause loss of steering control, damage to the hull, and possible injury to occupants. Any gear that is not carefully stowed or secured can take flight when maneuvering at high speeds. Constant alertness, a safe attitude and quick responses by the driver are at a premium. To be able to respond promptly, keep a hand on the throttle at all times.

Reducing Speed. When slowing down rapidly, steering control will initially be reduced because the boat's speed is not slowing as quickly as thrust is being reduced. In fact, if a boat traveling at high speed suddenly cuts its power, steering control may be lost completely. Whenever possible, put your boat on a straight course before slowing down.

Turning Maneuvers. During turning maneuvers, thrust from the propeller causes the boat to roll on its longitudinal axis. As the speed and tightness of a turn increases, the amount of roll increases. In a sharp turn with the boat rolled at a substantial angle, propellers on outboards and stern drives are closer to the water surface, which can result in air being drawn into its blades (sometimes referred to as *ventilation*). If the drive unit is trimmed up too much, it can aggravate this problem. When this occurs, there will be a sudden increase in engine rpm and loss of propeller power. To avoid possible damage to the engine and drive system, the rate of turn and/or speed should be reduced immediately.

High-Speed Stop. While it's recommended to gradually reduce boat speed before stopping, you may be faced with a situation where you need to stop quickly. If you are stopping to avoid an obstruction, the forward momentum of the boat could result in a collision. Also with this sudden decease in speed, you may lose steering control momentarily and the boat's wake could come over the transom and flood the well or cockpit. Use the high-speed stop to avoid these problems.
❶ Reduce throttle to idle rpm while making a sharp 90-degree turn.
❷ Shift into neutral after making the turn.

High-Speed Turn. Prior to making a high-speed turn, check to see that it is clear and safe to turn, and alert your passengers. Turn the wheel gradually and deliberately to maintain control throughout the maneuver. The greater the speed, the wider and more gradual the turn should be. If the turn is too sharp, the propeller will ventilate and turning control will be lost.

High-Speed Safety Tips
- *All occupants should be in seats and/or have a secure grip on boat.*
- *Attach lanyard to driver, if applicable.*
- *Keep one hand on the throttle and the other on the steering wheel.*
- *Maintain an alert lookout; don't get distracted.*
- *Use moderate and measured steering adjustments.*
- *Warn occupants of sudden changes in speed and direction.*
- *Avoid abrupt stops.*
- *If in doubt, slow down.*

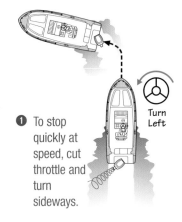

❷ Shift into neutral.

❶ To stop quickly at speed, cut throttle and turn sideways.

Turn Left

Returning to a Dock

To master this important maneuver you need to be aware of how your powerboat steers and reacts to changes of throttle and gearshift in different wind and current conditions. Here, your ability to maneuver at minimum control speed will play an important role. A common mistake, especially with boats that use directed thrust steering, is to oversteer at slow speeds, which result in loss of control of direction. It is far better to use small steering adjustments at minimum control speed with only an occasional brief, small increase in throttle to make a sharper turn. The critical time for a safe and successful docking usually starts as you make your final turn to come alongside the dock and ends as you reverse to stop the boat. Here, you'll need precise adjustment and coordination of throttle, gearshift and wheel (or tiller).

Key Points
- *Place fenders at dock level and prepare docklines before making the final approach.*
- *Be sure everyone knows in advance what to do with the docklines. Line handlers on the bow or deck should hold on or brace themselves against unexpected changes in direction or speed.*
- *Whenever possible, come alongside the dock with the bow pointing into the wind or current, whichever is stronger.*
- *Make your approach at minimum control speed, which will avoid or minimize damage should reverse suddenly not be available.*

Docking Tips
- *Minimum control speed allows you to make a smooth easy turn.*
- *Faster approach speeds require a more abrupt turn and timing becomes more critical.*
- *Always have an escape plan in case you misjudge your approach.*

Small-Angle Approach. This is the easiest approach to use because it requires only small adjustments of steering and power controls. It also accommodates temporary changes in wind conditions (unlike an approach parallel to the dock, which requires more precision and is less tolerant of changing conditions).

❶ Approach dock slowly at a 20 to 25 degree angle. If approach speed is too fast, shift into neutral to slow boat and use intermittent power to maintain minimum control speed.

❷ When bow is about ½ to 1 boat length away from dock, make a smooth turn to bring boat parallel and close to dock. As bow starts to turn, shift into neutral.

❸ Center wheel or tiller (or turn wheel toward dock if stern needs to be pulled in) and shift into reverse to stop boat.

❹ Shift to neutral. After boat is tied to dock, turn off engine.

Small-Angle Approach

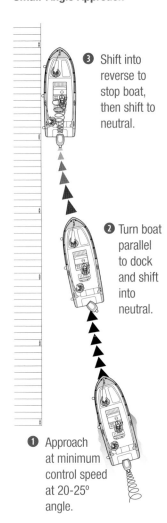

❸ Shift into reverse to stop boat, then shift to neutral.

❷ Turn boat parallel to dock and shift into neutral.

❶ Approach at minimum control speed at 20-25º angle.

Large-Angle Approach. In a situation where the wind pushes the boat away from the dock during its approach, you should increase your approach angle to head more into the wind. This increased angle will result in a tighter turn, which will increase the momentum of the swinging stern. If the stern swings too fast, you can prevent it from hitting the dock with a small turn of the wheel away from the dock as you reverse to stop the boat. As you come alongside, the wind will try to blow the boat away from the dock, so it is important to stop quickly and pass a line to the dock without delay. The best line to use is an after spring line fastened to the boat halfway (*amidships*) between the bow and stern and led aft to a dock cleat. If the boat starts to drift away before the other docklines are tied, you can put the boat in forward gear at idle rpm with the wheel turned away from the dock and the spring line will bring the boat alongside the dock again and hold it there. As the velocity of the wind increases, the power required to maintain minimum control speed will have to be increased to overcome the increased drag from windage, which reduces the forward speed of the boat.

❶ Approach dock at approximately 45° angle at a minimum control speed that maintains steering control against the wind.

❷ When bow is close to dock, turn boat almost parallel to dock, but maintain a small angle to compensate for the wind's tendency to push bow downwind.

❸ When bow is a couple of feet from dock, shift briefly into neutral and turn wheel toward dock, then shift into reverse and use a small amount of throttle to bring stern in as the boat stops.

❹ As soon as boat is alongside, shift into neutral and quickly tie after spring line. Then shift into forward with wheel turned away from dock to hold boat alongside until other docklines are secured. After boat is tied up, shift into neutral and turn off engine.

Downwind Docking. With the wind (or current) from astern, any use of the engine for steering may cause a faster approach speed, which will require more distance and reverse power to stop the boat. An increase in wind magnifies the problem. Once alongside the dock, the boat may drift rapidly down the dock or its stern spins out unless an after spring line fastened amidships on the boat is quickly looped over a dock cleat. If the line were led to the bow cleat, it could cause the stern to spin out from the dock.

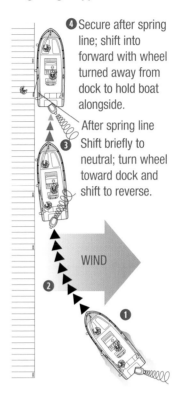

Large-Angle Approach

❹ Secure after spring line; shift into forward with wheel turned away from dock to hold boat alongside.

After spring line

❸ Shift briefly to neutral; turn wheel toward dock and shift to reverse.

WIND

Approach at minimum control speed at 45° angle.

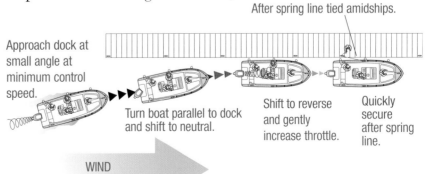

After spring line tied amidships.

Approach dock at small angle at minimum control speed.

Turn boat parallel to dock and shift to neutral.

Shift to reverse and gently increase throttle.

Quickly secure after spring line.

WIND

Returning to a Slip

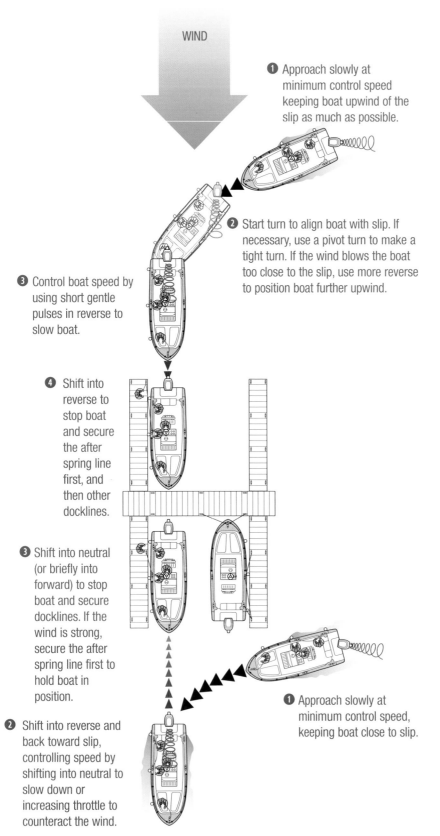

WIND

❶ Approach slowly at minimum control speed keeping boat upwind of the slip as much as possible.

❷ Start turn to align boat with slip. If necessary, use a pivot turn to make a tight turn. If the wind blows the boat too close to the slip, use more reverse to position boat further upwind.

❸ Control boat speed by using short gentle pulses in reverse to slow boat.

❹ Shift into reverse to stop boat and secure the after spring line first, and then other docklines.

❸ Shift into neutral (or briefly into forward) to stop boat and secure docklines. If the wind is strong, secure the after spring line first to hold boat in position.

❷ Shift into reverse and back toward slip, controlling speed by shifting into neutral to slow down or increasing throttle to counteract the wind.

❶ Approach slowly at minimum control speed, keeping boat close to slip.

Downwind Approach

Usually you will have more control going bow first into the slip. Controlling your speed will be your main concern as you will need to counteract the wind's effect of increasing the speed of the boat into the slip.

Upwind Approach

With this approach you can use the wind to help slow the boat as you bring it into the slip. Have docklines ready to help stop the boat from moving forward or backward too much in the slip.

Crosswind Approach. This approach demands precision boathandling and line handlers who know what to do. Determining the appropriate "crab" angle that will keep the boat lined up with the slip during the approach is the key to success. Allow enough distance in your approach to adjust the crab angle to suit the conditions.

❶ Approach slowly at minimum control speed and steer the boat at a "crab" angle so the path of the pivot point lines up with the slip.

❷ Pass the after spring line to the cleat on end of slip as bow approaches it.

❸ As soon as line is secured, turn boat parallel to the slip and shift into forward with the wheel turned away from the slip to hold the boat alongside until the other docklines are secured.

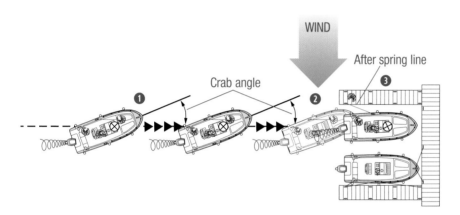

REVIEW QUESTIONS

1. To avoid having the stern of your boat swing into the dock, the recommended departure method is to _____ from the dock.

2. A type of turn frequently used in marinas and other confined spaces that turns a boat within a space of 1 to 2 boat lengths is called a _____.

3. When backing or turning in reverse, you should make _____ steering adjustments to maintain control of the boat.

4. To avoid the boat's wake from coming in over the transom when making a high-speed stop, you should reduce the throttle to idle rpm while making a sharp _____ turn.

5. When returning to a dock, you should make your approach with the bow into the _____ or _____ , whichever is stronger.

Answers: 1) back away 2) pivot turn 3) small 4) 90-degree 5) wind; current

7. Boathandling – Single-Screw with Rudder

KEY CONCEPTS
▶ Leaving & returning   ▶ Turning maneuvers

The boathandling maneuvers in this chapter apply for boats with a rudder and fixed propeller and will cover most situations. However, boats react differently in various wind and current conditions and it is best to practice these maneuvers with plenty of room before you need to use them in close quarters.

Leaving a Dock

CAUTION: Don't try to push a boat away from a dock using a hand or foot; if necessary, use a boat hook.

Back-Away Departure. For boats where prop walk will swing the stern toward the dock in reverse gear, you will need to use the rudder to counteract prop walk. As a boat gains backward speed, the rudder will become more effective allowing you to reduce rudder angle. If the prop walk force is too strong to overcome with the rudder, you will need to use a spring line (see Chapter 5). For boats where prop walk will swing the stern away from the dock, you can usually center the wheel and let prop walk do the turning.

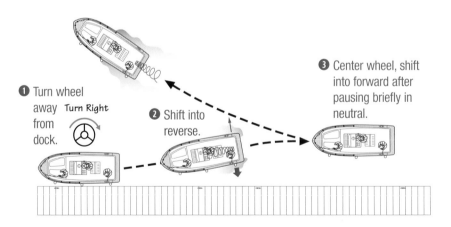

❶ Turn wheel away from dock. *Turn Right*

❷ Shift into reverse.

❸ Center wheel, shift into forward after pausing briefly in neutral.

Leaving a Slip

You usually can counteract the effect of prop walk by using the rudder to back out of a slip. If prop walk is too strong, you will need to twist (rotate) the boat before backing out by briefly going into forward to kick the stern out as in this example, or using a spring line (see Chapter 5). If the boat has a bow thruster, it can be used to align the boat with the slip as it backs out. In this example, the boat has a propeller that will "walk" the stern to port in reverse.

❶ Turn wheel and rudder to port and briefly shift into forward, just enough to swing stern to starboard without moving forward. Shift into neutral and allow pivoting momentum to continue until boat has pivoted enough to offset prop walk in reverse.

❷ Turn wheel and rudder to starboard and shift into reverse, slowly backing out. If prop walk swings boat too close to slip, shift into neutral and repeat steps ❶ and ❷.

❸ Turn boat once bow is clear of slip.

❹ Center wheel and shift into forward after pausing briefly in neutral.

Turning Maneuvers

When turning in close quarters, prop walk, wind and current need to be taken into account. If you have to make a turn through the wind, the direction of your turn could affect the turning arc and whether the boat's position ends up downwind or not. If your boat has a bow thruster, it can be used to tighten your turn. When making a tight pivot turn with a bow thruster, a touch of forward or reverse during the turn will hold your position in relation to the wind.

Pivot Turn Using Positive Prop Walk. Whenever possible you should make your turn in the direction that makes prop walk work for you – not against you. Turn clockwise for a boat with a right-hand propeller where the stern "walks" to port (clockwise) in reverse; and turn counterclockwise for a boat with a left-hand propeller which "walks" to starboard (counterclockwise) in reverse. You'll use a combination of prop walk and rudder force in your turn. Remember, water must be flowing past the rudder to generate a rudder force, and when you shift into forward gear, this generates water flow.

❶ Turn wheel hard over to starboard throughout the maneuver and shift into forward gear, adding a small, gentle amount of throttle to generate water flow over rudder to initiate turn.

❷ Before gaining headway, shift into reverse after pausing briefly in neutral. Prop walk will swing the stern to port.

❸ Shift into forward after pausing briefly in neutral.

❹ Shift into reverse and use prop walk again. Repeat steps until boat has completed its turn.

If your boat kicks its stern to starboard in reverse, then rotate the boat counterclockwise by reversing the direction of the wheel in step ❶.

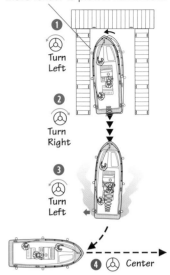

Move fender to protect hull at bow.

❶ Turn Left
❷ Turn Right
❸ Turn Left
❹ Center

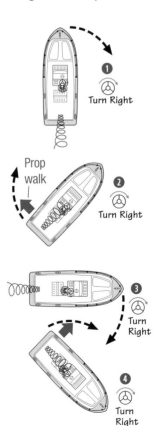

Clockwise Pivot Turn for Right-Hand Propeller

❶ Turn Right

Prop walk

❷ Turn Right

❸ Turn Right

❹ Turn Right

K-Turn Using Opposing Prop Walk. Whenever possible, you want to avoid this situation where prop walk is fighting your turn. You won't have to use a K-Turn if you have a bow thruster, but if you have to make this turn, allow more space for this K-Turn maneuver.

❶ For right-hand propeller, turn wheel hard over to port and shift into forward gear, adding a small punch of throttle to drive water over the rudder to start the boat turning to port.

❷ Shift into reverse, after pausing briefly in neutral, as you run out of space and keep wheel to port. Watch the rotation of the bow closely as prop walk slows the turn.

❸ When the bow stops its counterclockwise rotation, turn wheel to starboard and continue reversing as space allows.

❹ Shift to neutral, center wheel and shift into forward to slow boat's movement astern.

❺ Just before boat stops moving astern, turn wheel hard to port and give another punch of throttle. Repeat the sequence as necessary to complete the turn.

Driving Backward

When you are operating in close quarters, at some point you may have to back your boat. For boats with no bow thruster, the effect of prop walk will make steering a straight line difficult. You can use the rudder to counteract the turning tendency of prop walk, but with some boats prop walk will dominate. The following technique uses prop wash over the rudder created by momentary pulses in forward gear to keep the stern pointing in the direction you're aiming for. The illustration depicts a boat that "walks" to port in reverse.

❶ If the boat is aligned in the direction you want to back, turn wheel hard over to starboard and shift into reverse. As the boat moves astern, water flowing over the rudder will try to turn the stern to starboard, but prop walk may overpower the rudder's turning force.

❷ If there is room and enough momentum, shift to neutral to stop prop walk and allow the boat to steer using backward momentum and rudder alone.

❸ If there is not enough momentum and the direction of the boat's stern is to port of the intended direction, turn wheel to port and give a short burst of power in forward – just enough to initiate the rotation in the required direction; NOT to drive the boat forward.

❹ Shift to neutral and turn the wheel to starboard and reverse again. Repeat this sequence as necessary.

Key Points
- *Prop walk exists when the engine is in reverse or forward gear.*
- *Water must be flowing past the rudder to create a turning force.*

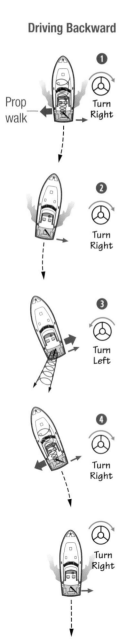

Driving Backward

Prop walk

❶ Turn Right

❷ Turn Right

❸ Turn Left

❹ Turn Right

Turn Right

Returning to a Slip

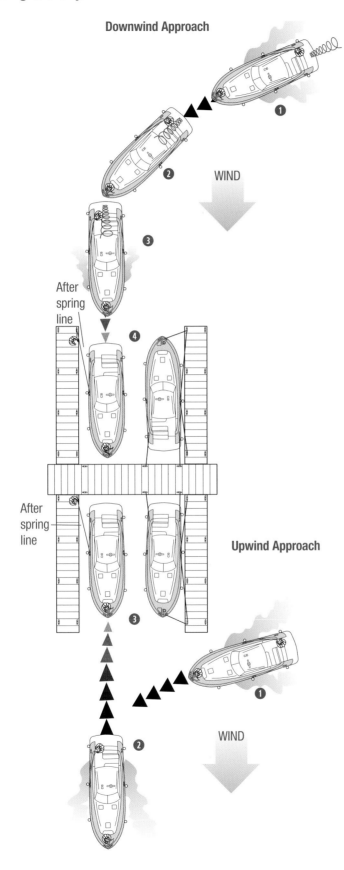

Downwind Approach

WIND

After spring line

After spring line

Upwind Approach

WIND

Downwind Approach

❶ Approach slowly at minimum control speed; keep boat upwind of slip as much as possible. Start turn to align boat with slip.

❷ Use a pivot turn to make a tight turn if necessary. If wind blows boat too close to slip, use more reverse to position boat further upwind.

❸ Control boat speed by using neutral and gentle applications of reverse.

❹ Shift into reverse to stop boat. Secure after spring line (fastened *amidships* on boat) first; then other docklines.

Upwind Approach

❶ Approach slowly at minimum control speed; keep boat close to slip. Turn to align boat with slip. Use a pivot turn if there is not enough space to make a normal turn.

❷ Shift into reverse and back toward slip, controlling speed by shifting into neutral to slow down or increasing throttle to counteract the wind.

❸ Shift into neutral or briefly into forward to stop the boat. Secure *amidships* after spring line first to hold boat in position; then other lines.

Crosswind Approach. This is a difficult maneuver, even for an experienced person, and should be practiced without using a bow thruster. If the wind is strong, you may find the bow thruster has little if any effect and can only be used for minor adjustments as the boat enters the slip. Another alternative is to ask for a more suitable docking space. Position fenders on both sides of the boat.

❶ Position boat downwind of the slip for a backing approach and shift into reverse.

❷ Make a backing turn toward the slip. The turn for smaller or lighter boats should be tighter than larger, heavier boats. Use rudder and gearshift to adjust for effects of prop walk and wind.

❸ Continue to back toward the windward side of the slip, making small adjustments with the rudder as necessary.

❹ Secure after spring line (fastened *amidships* on boat) and shift into forward with wheel turned to port to bring and hold boat alongside slip until starboard bow line and other docklines are secured.

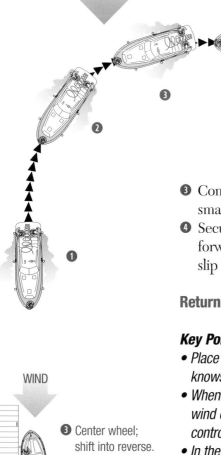

WIND

❸

❹

❷

❶

Returning to a Dock

Key Points
- *Place fenders at dock level and prepare docklines, making sure everyone knows what to do with them.*
- *Whenever possible, come alongside the dock with the bow pointing into the wind or current, whichever is stronger, making your approach at minimum control speed.*
- *In the absence of wind or current, approach the dock in a direction to take advantage of prop walk.*

Small-Angle Approach.

❶ Approach slowly at a 20 to 25 degree angle on the side that prop walk will pull your stern toward the dock in reverse.

❷ When the bow is about ½ to 1 boat length from dock, shift into neutral and make a smooth turn to bring boat close to dock and almost parallel. If more water flow over the rudder is needed to turn the boat, use intermittent power by briefly shifting into forward.

❸ When the bow is close to dock, center wheel and shift into reverse to stop. Prop walk will swing the stern into dock. If stern needs to be brought in more or faster, gently increase throttle.

WIND

❸ Center wheel; shift into reverse.

❷ Shift to neutral; turn boat almost parallel to dock.

❶ Approach at minimum control speed.

Crosswind Approach with Bow Thruster

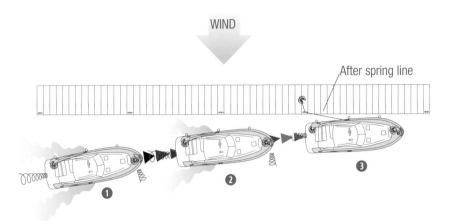

WIND

After spring line

❶ Approach at a small angle at minimum control speed. Use intermittent bursts of bow thruster to counteract the wind and keep boat on course.

❷ Reduce speed when close to dock, using bow thruster to prevent the bow from falling away from the dock.

❸ Secure the after spring line (fastened amidships on boat) and shift into forward with wheel turned away from dock to bring and hold boat alongside dock until other docklines are secured.

Close-Quarters Docking. Carefully check wind and current conditions before making this approach. If you feel uncomfortable about the dock space, look for another location. When possible, dock on the side that prop walk will pull the stern toward the dock when you reverse to stop forward momentum. Use the after spring line (fastened *amidships*) to bring the boat alongside as described in ❸.

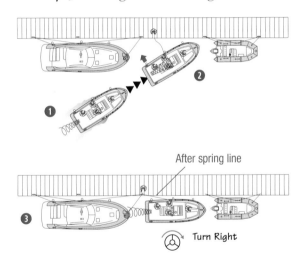

After spring line

Turn Right

❶ Approach slowly at minimum control speed at an angle to clear boat on port side.

❷ When the bow is close to dock, start to turn boat and pass after spring line to person on dock. Shift into reverse to stop boat and swing stern to dock.

❸ Secure after spring line and shift into forward with wheel turned away from dock to bring and hold boat alongside dock until other lines are tied.

REVIEW QUESTIONS

1. Prop walk occurs when the engine is in _____ or _____ gear.
2. _____ must be flowing past the rudder for it to be used for turning.
3. If a boat has a propeller where prop walk in reverse gear walks the stern to port, the best direction to make a pivot turn is _____.
4. When making a downwind approach to a slip, the first line to secure is the _____ spring line.
5. The preferred side to come alongside a dock is on the side of the boat that prop walk will pull the stern _____ the dock when the engine is in _____.

Answers: 1) reverse; forward 2) Water 3) clockwise 4) after 5) toward; reverse

8. Boathandling – Twin-Screws

KEY CONCEPTS
▶ Monohull maneuvers   ▶ Catamaran maneuvers

Twin-screw maneuvering concepts apply to both monohulls and catamarans. With a propeller in each hull of a catamaran, the distance between the two propellers is further apart and the twin-screw advantage is increased, but catamarans are generally lighter and have different windage and underwater profiles than a monohull. All boats react differently in wind and current and it is always best to practice maneuvers before you need to use them in close quarters.

MONOHULL MANEUVERS

Leaving a Dock

Back-Away Departure. With twin screws this is simply done by reversing the propeller closest to the dock to swing the stern away from the dock. Once the stern is clear, both propellers are reversed to back straight out. If conditions or other boats alongside the dock limit maneuvering space, then use an after spring line coupled with a pivot turn to rotate the stern until the boat can be backed straight out.

Sideways Maneuvering

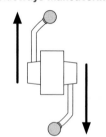

Split gearshifts with port in forward and starboard in reverse.

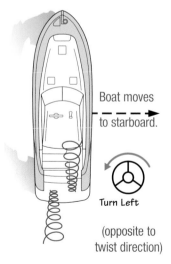

Boat moves to starboard.

Turn Left

(opposite to twist direction)

If boat twists too much and doesn't move sideways, try putting reversing propeller in neutral intermittently.

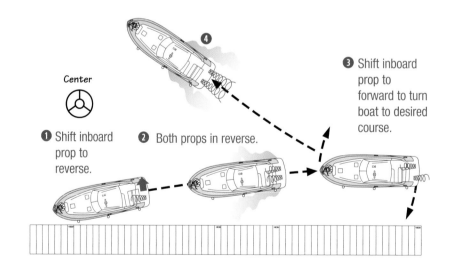

Center

❶ Shift inboard prop to reverse.

❷ Both props in reverse.

❸ Shift inboard prop to forward to turn boat to desired course.

Sideways Maneuvering. Many twin-screw boats with fixed propellers can be maneuvered sideways with varying degrees of success dependent on hull shape and configuration of propellers and rudders. The method described here may not work for all boats. Practice this maneuver to determine what works best for your boat.

Turning Maneuvers

Close-Quarters Maneuvering. At slow speeds, gearshifts are the primary controls used to maneuver twin-screw powerboats. In close-quarters maneuvering, the rudders generally remain centered.

Controlling Your Turn. You can vary your turn by using different combinations of gearshift and throttle. If you turn the steering wheel in the same direction as the turn, you will tighten the turn. Experiment with these controls in different wind and current conditions in open water to learn how your boat responds. Your goal is to be able to control your boat with precision when maneuvering around docks and slips.

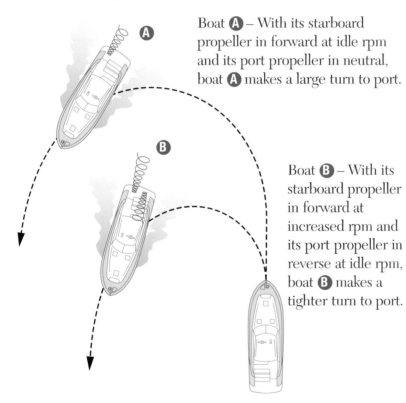

Boat **A** – With its starboard propeller in forward at idle rpm and its port propeller in neutral, boat **A** makes a large turn to port.

Boat **B** – With its starboard propeller in forward at increased rpm and its port propeller in reverse at idle rpm, boat **B** makes a tighter turn to port.

Backing Turn. With its port propeller in reverse at idle rpm and its starboard propeller in neutral, a boat will make a backing turn to the side opposite the reversing propeller or to starboard in this situation.

Pivot Turn. With its starboard propeller in forward at idle rpm and its port propeller in reverse at close to idle rpm, a boat will make a counterclockwise pivot (or twist) turn. The throttle on the reversing prop may have to be increased slightly to compensate for its reduced performance in reverse. If the boat starts to creep ahead, during a turn, either increase the throttle of the reversing propeller or put the forward propeller in neutral intermittently. If the boat creeps backward, increase the throttle of the forward propeller or shift the reversing propeller into neutral intermittently.

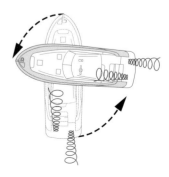

Returning to a Dock

❶ Approach slowly at minimum control speed.

❷ Make a smooth turn to bring boat almost parallel and close to dock by shifting outboard engine to neutral.

❸ Shift inboard prop to neutral and outboard prop in reverse to swing stern and stop boat. Reverse inboard prop, if necessary.

A twin-screw powerboat can be easily docked on either side.

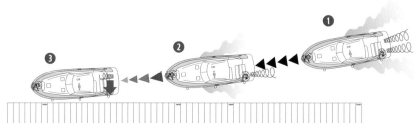

Returning to a Slip

❶ Approach slowly at minimum control speed.

❷ Make a pivot turn to line up boat stern first to slip.

❸ Shift both propellers into reverse at idle rpm and back into slip.

❹ Control speed and direction by shifting propellers to neutral as needed.

❺ Stop boat by briefly shifting into forward.

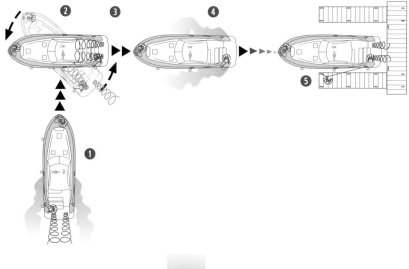

Crosswind Approach

❶ Position boat downwind of the slip for a backing approach and shift into reverse.

❷ Make a backing turn toward the slip with both engines in reverse and the starboard one at a higher throttle setting. Control the rate of turn with throttles and gearshifts. The turn for smaller or lighter boats should be tighter than for heavier ones.

❸ Secure the after spring line (fastened *amidships* on boat) and shift starboard propeller into forward with port propeller in neutral to bring and hold boat alongside slip until starboard bow line and other docklines are secured.

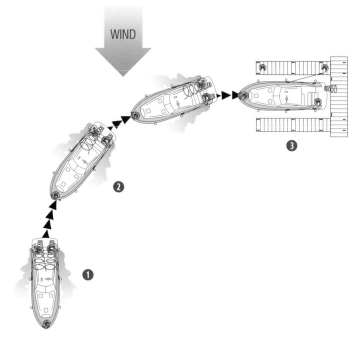

CATAMARAN MANEUVERS

Managing the "Four Corners." In a catamaran, the operator is managing a four-cornered box with two bows and two sterns and visibility can be a problem sometimes. The steering station may be located in several positions. Some are low and the person steering may be looking around parts of the cat. Others are higher, making it easier to see at least one side of the cat. In most cases, the person steering is not likely to have a good view of all four corners. It is very helpful to have a person serving as a lookout at these "blind spots."

Boathandling Considerations. Catamarans move forward and backward quite easily due to their long, narrow hulls. Their high topsides and cabins create a lot of windage and they don't coast very far into the wind. In fact, they could be considered to "stop on a dime." When maneuvering in an anchorage, windage can cause a cat to slide sideways into another boat. Current also has a significant effect on catamarans because they have two hulls. In close quarters maneuvering, gearshifts are typically the primary controls while rudders remain centered.

Effect of Dominant Force. If the dominant force of current or wind is on the bow or forward of the beam when leaving or returning to a dock, it is best to make a forward departure or return. If the dominant force is on the stern or aft of the beam, it is best to make a reverse departure or return. If the current and wind are in opposite directions, the one that has the dominant effect will determine whether it will be a forward or reverse departure or return.

Leaving a Dock

A catamaran can be easily pivoted from a dock by using opposite thrust with one engine in forward and the other in reverse. When pivoting, use a fender at the point of rotation on the hull to avoid damage. If there is no wind or current, simply put the engines in opposite thrust and use the rudders to "walk" the catamaran sideways.

Forward Departure. If the current (or wind) is strong, use a forward spring line to hold the cat in position while other docklines are released.

❶ Pivot bow from dock by shifting inboard engine in forward and outboard engine in reverse.
❷ Shift outboard engine in forward; adjust throttles as needed and stow fenders.

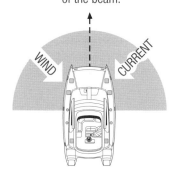

Forward Departure & Return
Dominant force is forward of the beam.

WIND   CURRENT

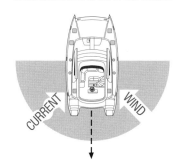

Reverse Departure & Return
Dominant force is aft of the beam.

CURRENT   WIND

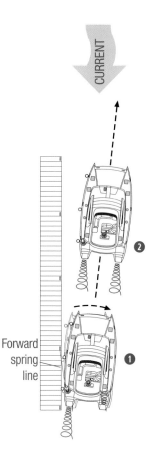

CURRENT

❷

Forward spring line   ❶

Reverse Departure

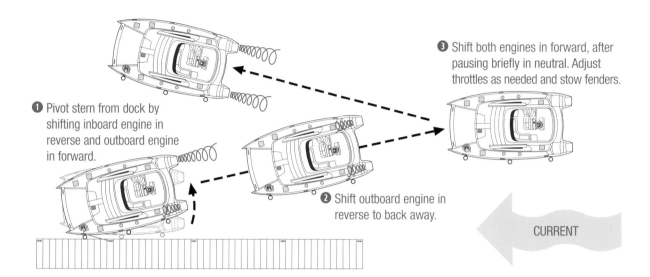

❸ Shift both engines in forward, after pausing briefly in neutral. Adjust throttles as needed and stow fenders.

❶ Pivot stern from dock by shifting inboard engine in reverse and outboard engine in forward.

❷ Shift outboard engine in reverse to back away.

CURRENT

Turning Maneuvers

To develop a mental picture of how a catamaran will respond to steering with twin engines, remember that if the driver pushes one of the throttles forward, that hull will move forward. Likewise, a throttle pulled into reverse will make that hull move backward. It may be helpful to picture turning someone by taking hold of the shoulders from behind, and pulling on one while pushing on the other.

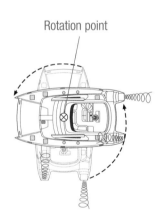

Rotation point

Pivot Turn. Because the engines are so far apart, it is easy to pivot a catamaran. With one engine in forward and the other in reverse, the cat will pivot in its own length.

Turn Around a Hull. By varying the amount of power of each engine, it is possible to pivot a catamaran around either hull.

Rotation point

Close Quarters Maneuvering. These pivoting characteristics make it easy to maneuver a catamaran. On most cats, the rudders will have little steering effect at low speeds and you will steer with the engines. Strong winds have a great effect on a cat because of its shallow draft and high topsides. Just as on other boats, the bows will blow away from the wind, often quickly. In close quarters, going forward may require more speed than is safe or comfortable, and the best way (sometimes the only way) in strong winds may be to back up towards the objective. When backing, keep the speed low and a firm hand on the wheel to prevent the rudders from accidentally turning hard over.

Returning to a Slip

Reverse Return. Unless the dominant force dictates otherwise, the preferred method is to back into a slip. It is much easier to disembark from the steps at the stern and twin-engine catamarans are just as maneuverable in reverse as they are with forward propulsion. Rig fenders on both sides and position the line handlers at the four corners to handle docklines and serve as lookouts for clearance with the slip.

Returning to a Dock

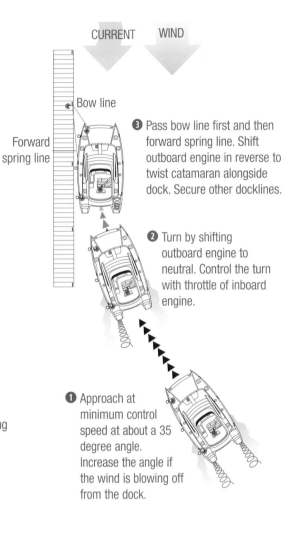

CURRENT WIND

Bow line

Forward spring line

❸ Pass bow line first and then forward spring line. Shift outboard engine in reverse to twist catamaran alongside dock. Secure other docklines.

❷ Turn by shifting outboard engine to neutral. Control the turn with throttle of inboard engine.

❶ Approach at minimum control speed at about a 35 degree angle. Increase the angle if the wind is blowing off from the dock.

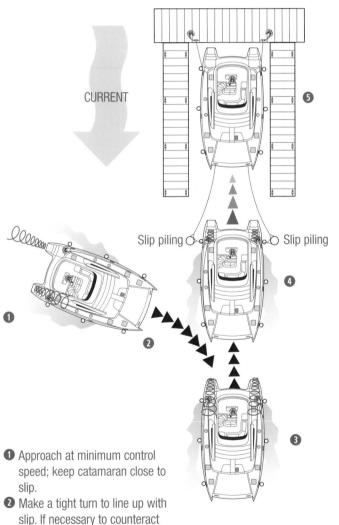

CURRENT

Slip piling   Slip piling

❶ Approach at minimum control speed; keep catamaran close to slip.
❷ Make a tight turn to line up with slip. If necessary to counteract set of current, increase throttle of reversing engine.
❸ Shift both engines into reverse and back toward the pilings, increasing the throttles or shifting into neutral as necessary for speed and steering control.

❹ Put loop end of bow lines over the pilings (or pick up line attached to each piling) and continue to back toward the slip.
❺ Pass stern lines and adjust bow and stern lines. Rig other docklines if necessary.

Crosswind Approach. This backing turn approach gives the operator control and flexibility in dealing with the effects of windage. There are other methods which may work just as well. Whatever method is used, you should practice it with plenty of room before you need to use it in a tight situation.

❶ Position catamaran downwind of the slip for a backing approach and shift into reverse.

❷ Make a backing turn toward the slip with both engines in reverse and the starboard one at a higher throttle setting. Control the rate of turn with throttles and gearshifts. The turn for smaller or lighter cats should be tighter than for heavier ones.

❸ Continue to back toward windward side of the slip, making adjustments with throttles and gearshifts as necessary.

❹ Secure the after spring line (fastened amidships on cat) and shift starboard engine into forward with port engine in neutral to bring and hold catamaran alongside slip until starboard bow line and other docklines are secured.

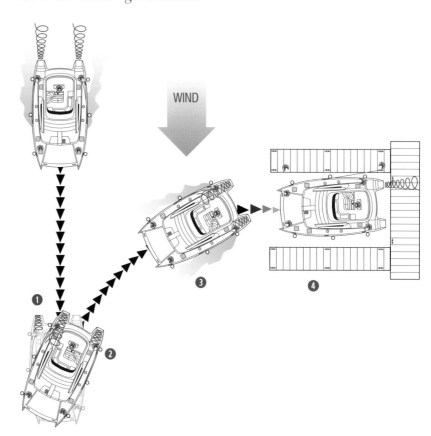

REVIEW QUESTIONS

1. When maneuvering a twin-screw boat in close quarters, _____ are the primary steering controls while _____ remain centered.
2. To make a pivot turn in a counterclockwise direction, shift the starboard engine in _____ and the port engine in _____.
3. To make a backing turn to starboard, shift the _____ engine in reverse and the _____ engine in neutral.
4. If the dominant force is forward of the beam of a catamaran, you should make a _____ departure when leaving a dock.
5. The preferred method for a catamaran to return to a slip is to _____ into it unless wind or current dictates otherwise.

Answers: 1) gearshifts; rudders 2) forward; reverse 3) port; starboard 4) forward 5) back

9. Advanced Boathandling

KEY CONCEPTS

▶ Anchoring   ▶ Heavy weather maneuvers
▶ Mooring   ▶ Bridges
▶ Coming alongside   ▶ Locks
▶ Rafting alongside

Advanced boathandling builds on the fundamental skills introduced in the previous chapters and enables you to deal with more challenging boating situations.

Anchoring

For a variety of reasons there will be times when you will anchor. Following are some procedures for setting and retrieving an anchor as well as information to help you select a suitable anchoring location.

Anchoring Tips
- *Check the water depth on a chart. If there is tide, make sure there is enough depth at low tide and enough* rode *(anchor line and chain) at high tide.*
- *Make sure there are no obstructions above or below the water that your boat could hit when it swings on its anchor.*
- *Try to anchor in calmer protected waters by choosing a location in the* lee *(downwind) of land or a breakwater.*

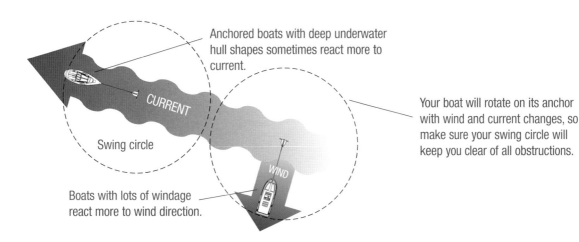

Anchored boats with deep underwater hull shapes sometimes react more to current.

Your boat will rotate on its anchor with wind and current changes, so make sure your swing circle will keep you clear of all obstructions.

Boats with lots of windage react more to wind direction.

- *Check your chart to avoid grassy or rocky bottoms which are difficult for setting lightweight anchors.*
- *Do not anchor in channels, high traffic areas or near underwater cables.*
- *Take a pass around the intended anchoring area to check for any uncharted hazards.*

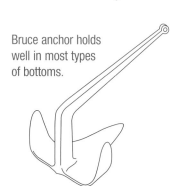

Lightweight-type anchor such as a Danforth holds well in sand, hard mud or soft clay bottoms, but are difficult to set in grass or rocky bottoms.

Bruce anchor holds well in most types of bottoms.

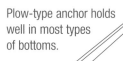

Plow-type anchor holds well in most types of bottoms.

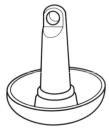

Mushroom anchor is best for mud and silt bottoms. Unlike other anchors shown here, it depends primarily on its weight for holding.

How well an anchor holds is determined by three primary factors:
• anchor type and size
• bottom type (i.e., mud, sand, clay), and
• the amount of scope, which is the ratio of length of rode to water depth plus height of bow (*freeboard*).

More scope increases holding ability. While a ratio of 5:1 may be adequate for an all-chain rode, or a nylon rode with a short length of chain for lunch in a sheltered spot with a good holding bottom, you'll want to increase it to 7:1 or more for strong wind and sea conditions.

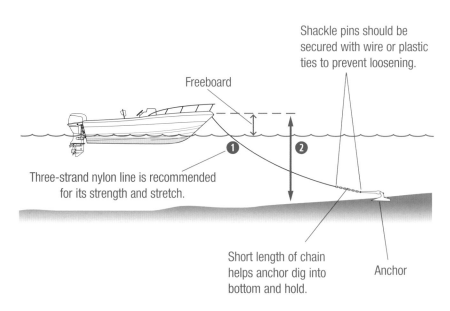

Shackle pins should be secured with wire or plastic ties to prevent loosening.

Freeboard

Three-strand nylon line is recommended for its strength and stretch.

Short length of chain helps anchor dig into bottom and hold.

Anchor

Example:
If water depth plus freeboard ❷ = 7 feet and if you let out 35 feet of rode ❶,

$$\text{Scope} = \frac{35 \text{ feet}}{7 \text{ feet}} = \frac{5}{1} \quad \text{or } 5:1$$

If the tide rises 3 feet, scope $= \dfrac{35 \text{ feet}}{10 \text{ feet}} = \dfrac{3.5}{1}$ or 3.5:1

and your anchor may drag unless you let out more line.

Anchor and Rode Inspection

☐ Check anchor line for worn or frayed areas.
☐ Check chain for damaged links.
☐ Check shackles are in good condition and pins are securely fastened.
☐ Check condition of anchor.

Setting an Anchor

When anchoring, a boat should be anchored at the bow. Anchoring at the stern could result in waves coming over the transom and possibly swamping smaller boats; plus there is a danger of carbon monoxide poisoning if the engine is running.

❶ After checking area, approach anchoring spot slowly, heading into wind or current, whichever is the dominant force on the boat.

❷ Stop boat and lower anchor over bow — do not throw it. The end of rode should be attached to boat before releasing anchor.

❸ Let out rode as boat drifts downwind. If wind has too little effect, back boat very slowly while letting rode run out freely. Avoid backing too fast, which could cause anchor to bounce along bottom.

❹ When a scope of 5:1 has been let out, secure the rode and reverse slowly against it until it becomes taut. Once anchor is set, let out additional rode as needed. To check whether anchor has set, hold a hand on the rode while reversing to feel for any chatter or vibration from anchor dragging or bouncing along bottom.

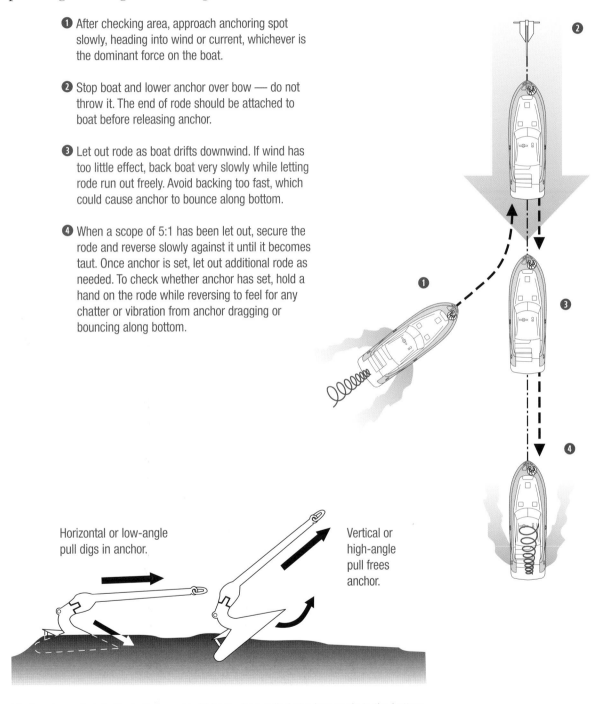

Horizontal or low-angle pull digs in anchor.

Vertical or high-angle pull frees anchor.

Most anchors dig into the bottom and hold best when pulled at a low angle to the bottom. A more vertical angle of pull can prevent the flukes from burying or even break the anchor free.

Catamaran Setting an Anchor

Bridles used for anchoring and mooring in their stowed position while underway.

CURRENT

❶ Approach the chosen anchor spot headed into the current or wind whichever is the dominant force on the catamaran.

❷ Stop the catamaran, and lower the anchor until it touches the bottom.

❸ Drift down current or downwind, letting out most of the intended scope. If the current or wind has too little effect, back the catamaran very slowly while letting out the rode.

❹ Snub the rode by stopping the windlass and reverse slowly until the rode is taut and the anchor is holding. When the anchor appears to be set, increase the engine RPMs to 1500 to check that it is a "true" set. Once the anchor is set, let out additional scope appropriate to the type of rode and conditions.

Bridle

❺ Attach the bridles to the anchor rode. Then let out additional rode until the bridles take the load, and a short length of rode hangs between the bridle attachment point and the anchor roller.

Retrieving an Anchor

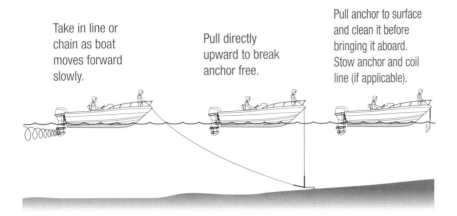

Take in line or chain as boat moves forward slowly.

Pull directly upward to break anchor free.

Pull anchor to surface and clean it before bringing it aboard. Stow anchor and coil line (if applicable).

Control button

A windlass should be used to raise the anchor and its rode, not to break the anchor free.

Windlass. Larger boats usually use a windlass for raising the anchor, which can handle both line and chain. Powerboats typically use electric windlasses operated by a button in the windlass or deck, or by a hand control. It's a good idea to run your engine while using an electric windlass to avoid running down the batteries. When lowering chain, use the brake to stop it, not your hand.

Keep clothing, hair and other body parts clear of the windlass. Never put a hand on the chain while the windlass power is on.

Hand Signals. The noise of engine, wind and waves makes it difficult to communicate by voice. Hand signals are a good alternative, but the driver and bow person should review them beforehand.

Raise left arm with hand pointing to port (left) to indicate steer to port.

Raise right arm with hand pointing to starboard (right) to indicate steer to starboard.

Raise arm and motion forward to indicate go straight ahead.

Raise arm with closed fist to indicate stop.

Raise arm with palm facing aft to indicate reverse.

Mooring

Moorings typically have a large buoy that is attached to an anchor on the bottom with chain. They often have a floating line *(pennant)*, sometimes rigged with a pickup pole, which you can grab to bring the pennant aboard. If there is no pole or you cannot reach it, you will need a boat hook. Some moorings may not have a pennant and you'll need to tie a stout line to the chain or the ring on the bottom of the buoy, using two round turns to reduce chafe. Buoys may have a ring on top, but before tying onto it make sure a metal rod connects it to the bottom ring. A ring attached only to the buoy's surface could rip off.

Picking Up a Mooring. The driver should approach the mooring with it on his side of the boat to keep it in sight throughout the approach. If the driver loses sight of the mooring, the bow person should use hand signals and a boat hook to direct the driver.

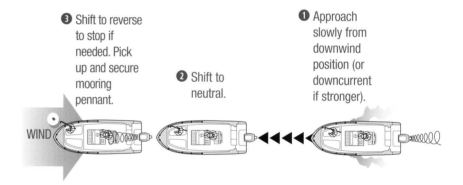

❸ Shift to reverse to stop if needed. Pick up and secure mooring pennant.

❷ Shift to neutral.

❶ Approach slowly from downwind position (or downcurrent if stronger).

WIND

Departure

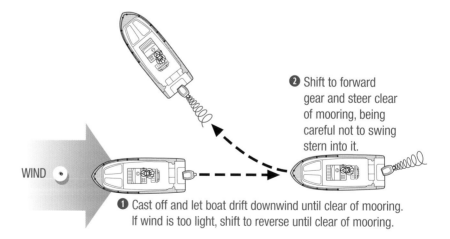

❷ Shift to forward gear and steer clear of mooring, being careful not to swing stern into it.

WIND

❶ Cast off and let boat drift downwind until clear of mooring. If wind is too light, shift to reverse until clear of mooring.

Catamaran Picking Up a Mooring Bow Approach

WIND

❸ Pass a bridle line from each bow through the eye splice of the pennant and lead it back to the bow from which it came. Adjust the bridles as necessary.

❷ Stop the catamaran, and a line handler picks up the mooring pennant with a boat hook.

❶ Approach the mooring into the wind (or current whichever one is the dominant force) on the side closest to the driver.

Catamaran Picking Up a Mooring Stern Approach

WIND   CURRENT

❻ Adjust the length of both lines as necessary.

❺ The free end of the first bow line is cleated to the bow cleat on the steering station side. Both ends of the second bow line are cleated to the bow cleat on the opposite side.

❹ Allow the boat to drift back as both line handlers walk forward with the lines.

❸ Pass the end of the first bow line through the ring (or pennant) and hand it to the other line handler. Pass the second bow line through the ring (or pennant) keeping both ends on board.

❷ Approach the mooring on the steering station side by backing into the wind or current whichever one is the dominant force. Once the cat is lined up with the mooring and getting close to it, use the engine further away from the mooring to make the final approach to keep the pennant from fouling in the near propeller.

❶ Rig a bow line from the bow cleat on the steering station side and lead it aft outside all lifelines to the stern steps.

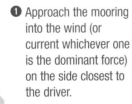

Coming Alongside an Anchored Boat

❶ Determine swing behavior of anchored boat and approach slowly at an appropriate angle. When boat is about half to one boat length away, make smooth turn to bring boat parallel to anchored boat and shift to neutral.

❷ Reverse to stop boat. If necessary, increase throttle to accelerate swing, especially if anchored boat starts to swing away. Shift to neutral and tie up.

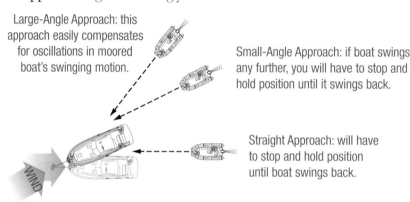

Effect of Wind Shifts on Coming Alongside. Generally, anchored boats point into the wind unless the current is dominant. Determine the amount and quickness of the anchored boat's oscillations and adjust your approach angle accordingly.

Large-Angle Approach: this approach easily compensates for oscillations in moored boat's swinging motion.

Small-Angle Approach: if boat swings any further, you will have to stop and hold position until it swings back.

Straight Approach: will have to stop and hold position until boat swings back.

Rafting Alongside

Always wait to be invited and use your own fenders.

❶ First boat sets anchor.

❷ Bring the second boat alongside with fenders in place, and secure to the first boat with spring, bow and stern lines.

❸ Set additional anchors as needed. If a wind shift is anticipated, set an anchor 60 degree angle to the first anchor from the second boat.

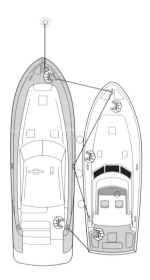

Rafting lines should be secured so they can be easily removed in case of an emergency.

Rafting Checklist

☐ Place fenders high enough to protect topsides.

☐ To cross over boats, get onto a boat at its maximum beam location, then walk around the foredeck to get to the maximum beam on the other side of the boat.

☐ Be considerate of other people's quiet hours after dark.

☐ Inform other boats of your departure plans.

Heavy Weather Maneuvering

Smaller outboards are usually designed for use in relatively sheltered waters. If caught unexpectedly in bad weather or rough seas, position people and equipment as low and as close to the center of the boat as possible. Don't let water accumulate in the cockpit or bilge. A cockpit half full of water in severe sea conditions is a cause for concern.

Keep in mind that you want to work your boat through the waves while always maintaining control and minimizing stress on the boat. Avoid slamming into waves or falling off their backsides by making adjustments in direction and throttle to anticipate and react to changing wave conditions. Remember, one hand on the wheel and one hand on the throttle.

Running Against Wind and Waves. As waves increase in size, it is usually better not to pound straight into them, but to cross them at an angle to produce an easier ride for the boat and its occupants. This angle will vary from 10 degrees to 45 degrees, depending on the size of the waves. Often waves seem to come in a recurring pattern with a couple of smaller ones followed by a larger one, then a couple of smaller ones followed by a larger one, etc. Sometimes, it is just a matter of slowing down a little to let the boat ride over the large wave. Other times, you may have to increase your angle to the large wave and slow down. Once it passes, you can go back to your previous direction and throttle setting.

Running With Wind and Waves. When strong winds and large waves are coming from behind, there is a risk of running down the front side of a wave and burying the bow in the backside of the next wave. To avoid this situation, run at slower speed to match the speed of the waves, maintaining a position just behind the crest.

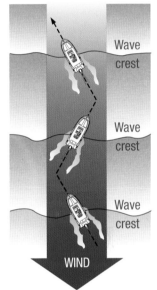

If your destination is directly upwind in heavy seas, you can "tack" (zig-zag) across waves for a smoother ride.

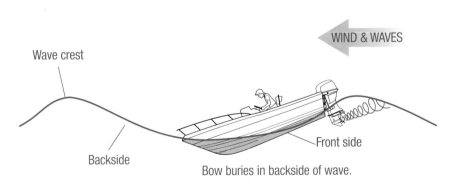

Bow buries in backside of wave.

Safety Tip for Inlets
Large waves are frequently encountered in inlets, especially with an outgoing (ebbing) current and wind blowing onshore. If the inlet is too rough, it's safer to remain offshore and wait for slack water or less wind.

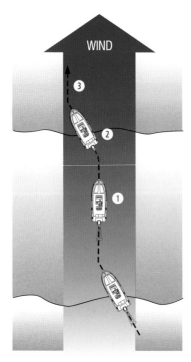

❶ Steer straight up the backside of a wave.

❷ As you near the wave top, steer at an angle to stay in contact with the wave as you pass over it.

❸ As you near the end of the front side of the wave, straighten your course to steer up the backside of the next wave.

Another situation to avoid is jumping off wave tops at high speed and making a hard landing, which could injure people on board or cause damage to the boat. You should run at a slower speed to get a softer ride. In large waves, which are widely spaced apart and not breaking, you can work your way through them by angling over the wave top to avoid falling off them (left).

Running Sideways to Wind and Waves. Running sideways to wind and waves will give you a softer ride, but as waves get larger there is a risk of the boat rolling over or corkscrewing out of control.

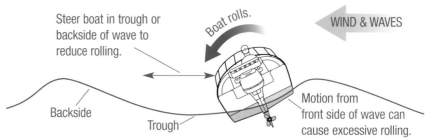

Bridges

Lights. Bridges are lighted from sunset to sunrise and during reduced visibility. Red lights typically indicate unsafe areas, and green lights indicate areas safe for navigation.

Fixed bridges are marked as follows:
• Two green lights mark the center of a navigable channel.
• A red light marks each margin of a navigable channel or each pier if it limits the channel margin.
• Three vertical white lights directly above each green light marks the main channel span if there are two or more spans over a navigable channel.

Bridges that can be opened are marked as follows:
• Red lights mark a closed bridge and the piers of a bridge.
• Green lights mark a bridge when it is open.

Drawbridges may open on a fixed schedule or on demand. A request for an opening may be made by calling the bridge tender on VHF Channels 13 or 16 (or Channel 9 in FL, GA, SC) using the name of the bridge, or by sound signals.
• One prolonged blast and one short blast indicates a request to open a bridge. If the bridge can be opened immediately, the bridge tender will respond with one prolonged blast and one short blast.
• Five short blasts by the bridge tender indicates the bridge cannot be opened immediately, or if opened, will be closed promptly.

Locks

Locks are a means of allowing a boat to pass around a dam or from a different water level to another. Many locks have an on-duty lockmaster who controls all movement through the locks, sometimes using horn or light signals and/or VHF radio (Channel 13).

Light Signals
Green = enter lock
Yellow (often flashing) =
    prepare to move into lock
Red = do not enter

Horn Signals
One long blast = enter lock
One short blast = leave lock

A boat entering a lock should have fenders in place and adequate lengths of line coiled and ready to use. Boats may "lock-through" alongside a lock wall or in the center of the chamber tied off on both sides. Once secured, lock instructions may require that the engine be turned off. With large changes of water level, the water in the lock may become quite turbulent when the water rises in the lock. Never use hands or feet to hold onto or fend off the lock wall.

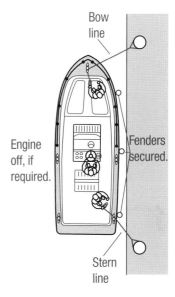

Maintain tension on bow and stern lines as the water level in the lock changes.

REVIEW QUESTIONS

1. Your boat has a two-foot freeboard. You wish to anchor on a windy day in 18 feet of water. Your anchor rode (line plus chain) should be at least _____ feet long.
2. When setting an anchor, you should let out the _____ as the boat drifts downwind. If the wind has too little effect, back the boat very _____.
3. Large waves are frequently encountered in inlets, especially with a/an _____ (outgoing) current and onshore wind. If the inlet is too rough, it is safer to wait for _____ water or less wind.
4. A _____ light at a lock signals do not enter the lock.
5. Two _____ lights on a fixed bridge mark the _____ of a navigable channel.

10. Equipment & Requirements

KEY CONCEPTS

▶ Registration, documentation & numbering

▶ Hull identification

▶ Maximum capacities

▶ Safety equipment

▶ Federal regulations

▶ Pollution

▶ Accident reporting

Part of preparation is making sure you have equipment on board that works properly and conforms to federal and state requirements. Once you leave the dock, you'll be sharing the waters with other boaters and enjoying the natural environment. Safety and seamanship includes knowing and observing the regulations that help protect the waters and govern safe operation.

Registration, Documentation & Numbering

Registration & Documentation. A powerboat must either be registered in its state of principal use, or federally documented. The certificate of registration or certificate of documentation must be aboard the vessel when it is operated, and just as with an automobile registration, must be produced if requested by a law enforcement officer. If documented, the hailing port must be displayed on the stern and the documentation number must be permanently affixed to the inside of the hull. If registered, the state registration number must be displayed on each side of the bow of the boat in block letters at least three inches high and have a contrasting color from the background color.

Hull Identification Number (HIN). Boats manufactured after November 1, 1972 are required to display a Hull Identification Number in two locations on the boat. The primary number must be near the top on the starboard (right) side of the transom. In 1984 a second location of the HIN was required and it is located somewhere in the interior of the boat or beneath a fitting or hardware. The HIN is also on the certificate of registration or documentation, but keep a record of this number to identify your boat in case it is stolen.

Maximum Capacities Label or Plate. All powerboats (except inflatables) smaller than 20 feet in length built after October 31, 1972 must have a legible U.S. Coast Guard capacities label permanently displayed and visible to the operator. For boats less than 20 feet long with no capacities label/plate, a rough guide is to multiply the length (in feet) by the beam (in feet) and divide by 15 to get a maximum number of people.

State decal — its location will vary by state.

State registration number

State registration numbers must be on both sides of the bow and lettering must be at least three inches high. The space between groupings of letters and numbers is equal to a letter width (except for "I" or "1").

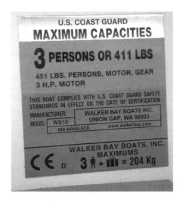

Required Equipment

The Federal Boating Safety Act of 1971 and subsequent regulations specify the equipment a powerboat must carry based on a boat's overall length. You should also check your state's boating regulations.

Life Jackets

At least one wearable life jacket (Type I, II, III, or V) of appropriate size for each person on board is required. Under federal regulations, children under 13 years of age are required to wear an approved life jacket while underway unless below deck or in an enclosed cabin. States may have different age requirements which should be observed while operating in state waters. Life jackets must be readily accessible, not buried under other gear or stowed in plastic bags in locked compartments. Any boat 16 feet long or larger must also carry at least one throwable device (Type IV) which should be readily available. Life jackets must be U.S. Coast Guard approved, marked with a Type designation, and be in good condition. Regularly check all life jackets on board for loose stitching, rips, frayed straps or fabric and jammed zippers. Also ensure inflatable life jackets are maintained according to the manufacturer's instructions. Replace any that are no longer in good condition.

Type I Life Jacket (Offshore) is designed to turn an unconscious person from a face down position to a vertical or slightly backward position and maintain that position. The adult size provides a minimum of 22 pounds of flotation and the child size provides 11 pounds of buoyancy. The Type I life jacket is suitable for all waters, but is the bulkiest and most uncomfortable to wear.

Type II Life Jacket (Near-Shore Vest) is designed to turn some unconscious people over, but the turning action is not as reliable or as pronounced as the Type I. Its adult size has a minimum of 15.5 pounds of flotation and it comes in four sizes based on the weight of the wearer. Type II is suitable for calm, inland waters and is relatively uncomfortable to wear.

Type III Life Jacket (Flotation Aid) is not designed to turn an unconscious person over and is used in a variety of sports such as boating, skiing, hunting, kayaking, etc. It comes in a wide variety of sizes and colors and is the most popular and comfortable type of life jacket. Type III is good for a conscious person in calm, inland waters.

Type IV Throwable Devices are designed to throw to a person in the water to hold onto (not worn) until rescued. This Type includes boat cushions, life rings and horseshoe buoys.

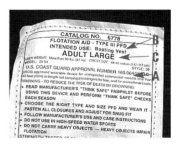

U.S. Coast Guard approval notice (A) on a life jacket includes Type designation (B) and size (C).

Type I Life Jacket

Type II Life Jacket

Type III Life Jacket

Type IV Throwable Device

Type V
Life
Jacket

Type V
Belt Pack
Inflatable
Life Jacket

Type V
Life Jacket
(Float Coat)

Type V Life Jackets are designed for specific activities and may be carried instead of another life jacket subject to the conditions specified on the label. If the label says the life jacket is "approved only when worn," it must be worn to meet the one life jacket per person requirement. When inflatable Type Vs are inflated, their performance is equal to a Type I, II, or III as noted on the label (also check the label for USCG approval). Type V Hybrid life jackets have a small amount of inherent buoyancy in addition to the buoyancy created when their inflatable chamber is activated. The wide variety of Type Vs includes deck suits, "float coats," work vests and inflatable vests.

Inflatable vests are considered the most comfortable of all life jackets. Regularly check the CO_2 cartridge to make sure its seal hasn't been punctured. If it has, there will be no CO_2 to inflate the life jacket. Always carry at least one backup cartridge. Once a year you should check your life jacket for leaks by inflating it with the oral inflation tubes and leaving it overnight.

Signaling Equipment

Visual Distress Signals (VDS). All boats operating in U.S. coastal waters, the Great Lakes, territorial seas and those waters connected directly to them up to a point where they narrow to less than two miles are required to carry USCG approved visual distress signals. Powerboats less than 16 feet or boats participating in organized events are not required to carry day signals but must carry night signals when operating from sunset to sunrise.

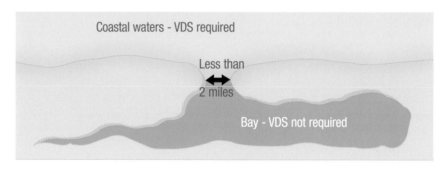

Coastal waters - VDS required

Less than
2 miles

Bay - VDS not required

There are a variety of visual distress signals available for day use, night use and for both. If pyrotechnic devices (flares, smoke signals, meteors) are selected, a minimum of three signals for day use and three signals for night use, or three signals approved for both day and night are required. All distress flares must not have exceeded their service life and must be kept in an accessible location. A watertight red or orange container labeled "Distress Signals" is recommended.

Distress Signals. The following signals can only be used to indicate a vessel is in distress and requires assistance. If a vessel has a life-threatening emergency, it can use a "Mayday" call on a VHF radio as a distress signal. Chapter 11 describes how to make a Mayday call.

Day Use Only
• orange smoke signal
• continuous sounding of fog horn
• orange distress flag (black square & black circle on orange)
• slowly raising & lowering arms
• Intl. code flags "N" over "C"
• square flag above or below a ball

Night Use Only
• electric automatic SOS distress light (ordinary flashlight does not meet requirement)

Day & Night Use
• handheld red flare
• parachute red flare
• red-star meteor shells

Safety Tip
If visual distress signals are not legally required for your area, it is good seamanship to carry them on board in case an emergency arises.

Signals to Attract Attention. Light and sound signals may be used to attract attention as long as they cannot be mistaken for distress signals, limited visibility signals or signals used when meeting another vessel (see Chapter 13 for information on these signals). A searchlight may also be aimed in the direction of danger.

Sound Signaling Device. You are required to carry a sound signaling device that is capable of making an efficient sound signal. If your boat is 39.4 feet (12 meters) or larger, you must carry a bell as well as a whistle.

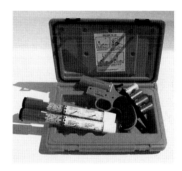

A watertight flare kit is recommended to meet visual distress signal requirements.

Navigation Light Equipment

Any boat operating between sunset and sunrise, and during restricted visibility, must display lights. Lighting requirements vary considerably with the size and type of vessel (see Chapter 13 for more information).

Fire Extinguishers

Fire extinguishers are classified by the type of fire they are designed to extinguish and by their size. The letter indicates the type of fire: "A" for combustible solids like wood, paper, cloth, rubber and some plastics; "B" for flammable liquids such as gasoline, diesel, oil, grease and alcohol; and "C" for live electrical fires. Some extinguishers can be approved for several different types of fire and are labeled accordingly. The Roman numeral, which follows the letter, designates the size of the extinguisher: "I" being the smallest and "V" the largest. U.S. Coast Guard approved fire extinguishers are required if any of the following conditions exist:
• inboard engine installed
• closed compartments or under-seat compartments where portable fuel tanks may be stored

Fire extinguishers should be readily accessible and mounted away from possible sources of fire.

Additional Equipment

In addition to the required equipment, most boats will need other items suitable to the intended use of the boat and available stowage space, such as:

- Anchor & rode
- Towline
- First Aid kit
- Heaving line
- Bailer/bilge pump
- Oars/paddles (for small powerboats)
- Tool kit
- Spare parts
- Boat hook
- Chart of area
- Boarding ladder
- Compass
- Flashlight
- VHF radio and/or cellular phone
- Spotlight
- Fenders
- Binoculars
- Docklines
- GPS

- double bottoms not sealed to the hull or not completely filled with flotation material
- closed living spaces
- closed stowage compartments in which combustible or flammable materials are stored
- permanently installed fuel tank(s), which could not be moved in the event of a fire or other emergency.

The minimum number of hand portable fire extinguishers (B1 or B2) required on a recreational boat is based on the overall length of the boat.

Length	No Fixed System	With Approved Fixed System*
Under 26'	one B-I	None
26 – 40'	two B-I or one B-II	one B-I
40 – 65'	three B-I or one B-II & one B-I	two B-I or one B-II

* An approved fixed system is an U.S. Coast Guard approved pre-engineered fire extinguishing system installed for the protection of the engine compartment.

Inspect fire extinguishers monthly to ensure: seals are intact, there is no physical damage, and that indicators are functional and reading in the desired range. Fire extinguishers should be placed where they are readily accessible and away from possible sources of fire.

Ventilation

All boats with gasoline engines are required to have a natural ventilation system for each compartment that contains an engine or fuel tank. A natural ventilation system consists of a supply duct for fresh air flow and an exhaust duct. A powered ventilation system with one or more exhaust blowers is required for each compartment that has an inboard gasoline engine with a starter motor. Boats required to have an exhaust blower will have a warning label close to the ignition switch stating that before starting the engine, the blower must be operated for at least four minutes.

Air Circulation in Bilge and Engine Compartment

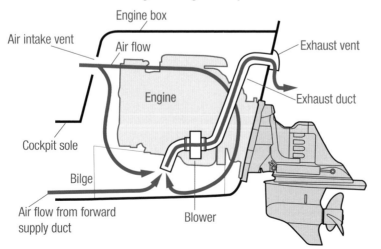

Backfire Flame Arrestors

All inboard gasoline engines must have a U.S. Coast Guard approved carburetor backfire flame arrestor on each carburetor to prevent the risk of fire if a backfire occurs. These flame arrestors should be routinely cleaned.

Minimum Required Safety Equipment

A flame arrestor controls a backfire flame should it occur. Use only a flame arrestor suitable for marine use.

Equipment	Class A < 16 ft.	Class 1 16 to < 26 ft.	Class 2 26 to < 40 ft.	Class 3 40 to 65 ft.
Life Jackets	One Type I, II, III or V wearable life jacket for each person on board or being towed on water skis, plus one Type IV throwable device for boats 16 feet and over.			
Whistle or a sounding device, such as a horn	Vessels less than 39.4 ft. (12 meters) must carry an efficient sound-producing device.		Vessels 39.4 ft. (12 meters) or longer must carry a whistle.	
Bell	Not required on Class A, Class 1 or Class 2 vessels.		Vessels 39.4 ft. (12 meters) or longer must carry a bell.	
Fire Extinguishers	One B-1 Type extinguisher. Not required on outboard boat less than 26', or boat is open construction and has no permanent fuel tanks.		Two B-1 fire extinguishers, or one B-II type fire extinguisher.	Three B-1 fire extinguishers, or one B-1 and one B-II fire extinguishers.
Visual Distress Signals (coastal waters only)	Required only when operating at night.	Signals for day and night use are required. Examples are: orange smoke signal (day) and S-O-S electric light (night); or three red flares (day/night).		

Water Pollution

The Refuse Act of 1899 prohibits throwing, discharging or depositing any refuse matter of any kind (trash, garbage, oil, etc.) into the waters of the United States.

Garbage Management. Under the Provisions of MARPOL, Annex V, limitations are placed on the discharge of garbage from vessels. It is illegal to dump plastic anywhere in the ocean or navigable waters of the United States. It is illegal to discharge garbage in the navigable waters of the United States including the inland waters and the Great Lakes. States and local laws may have additional restrictions. Vessels 26 feet or longer must display in a prominent place, a durable placard

Discharge of Garbage

U.S Navigable Water to 3 Miles from Shore:
Illegal: Plastic; any garbage
Legal: Greywater (shower, sinks); dishwater

3 to 12 Miles from Shore:
Illegal: Plastic.
If 1 square inch or larger: food, waste, paper, rags, glass, crockery, metal, dunnage
Legal: Greywater; dishwater.
If smaller than 1 square inch: food, waste, paper, rags, glass, crockery, metal

12 to 25 Miles from Shore:
Illegal: Plastic; dunnage
Legal: Greywater; dishwater; food waste; paper; rags; glass; crockery; metal

DISCHARGE OF OIL PROHIBITED

THE FEDERAL WATER POLLUTION CONTROL ACT PROHIBITS THE DISCHARGE OF OIL OR OILY WASTE INTO OR UPON THE NAVIGABLE WATERS OF THE UNITED STATES, OR THE WATERS OF THE CONTIGUOUS ZONE, OR WHICH MAY AFFECT NATURAL RESOURCES BELONGING TO, APPERTAINING TO, OR UNDER THE EXCLUSIVE MANAGEMENT AUTHORITY OF THE UNITED STATES, IF SUCH DISCHARGE CAUSES A FILM OR DISCOLORATION OF THE SURFACE OF THE WATER OR CAUSES A SLUDGE OR EMULSION BENEATH THE SURFACE OF THE WATER. VIOLATORS ARE SUBJECT TO SUBSTANTIAL CIVIL PENALTIES AND/OR CRIMINAL SANCTIONS INCLUDING FINES AND IMPRISONMENT.

Discharge of Oil Prohibited

The Federal Water Pollution Control Act prohibits the discharge of oil or oily waste upon or into any navigable waters of the United States. This prohibition includes any discharge that causes a film or discoloration of, the surface of the water, or causes a sludge or emulsion beneath the surface of the water. Violators are subject to substantial civil and/or criminal sanctions, including fines and imprisonment.

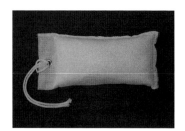

Oil absorbent pad

of at least 4 inches by 9 inches notifying passengers and crew of these restrictions. Offshore vessels 40 feet or longer with a galley and berths must have a written waste management plan and a designated person responsible for it.

Oil or Hazardous Material Pollution. The Federal Water Pollution Control Act prohibits the discharge of oil or hazardous substances that may be harmful to U.S. navigable waters. All mechanically powered vessels are required to retain oily mixtures on board and draining oil or oily waste into the bilge is prohibited. Spilled or leaking oil usually end up in the bilge and it is against the law to pump bilge water overboard if it is contaminated. Acceptable methods of retention of oily or hazardous mixtures for disposal at a reception facility ashore include: oil absorbent pads or sheets, buckets, bailers, and plastic bags. Vessels 26 feet or longer must display an Oil Discharge Prohibited placard of at least 5 inches by 8 inches in machinery spaces or at the bilge pump station.

If a vessel discharges oil or a hazardous substance in the water, the operator or owner must immediately notify the U.S. Coast Guard at a toll free number: 800-424-8802. The following information must be reported: location, source, substance, description, color, size, date and time observed.

Sewage Pollution. The Clean Water Act prohibits the discharge of untreated or inadequately treated sewage into the navigable waters of the United States, which includes coastal waters up to three miles offshore. The Act established "No-Discharge Zones" (NDZs) where the discharge of any treated and untreated sewage is prohibited. Freshwater lakes and reservoirs are NDZs. The EPA maintains a list of no-discharge zones, which is available online.

ONLINE... NDZs: http://water.epa.gov/polwaste/vwd/vsdnozone.cfm

Installed toilets (*heads*) on all vessels must be U.S. Coast Guard approved Type I, II, or III marine sanitation devices (MSDs), which are designed to treat, discharge or retain sewage. This requirement does not apply to portable toilets (heads). Type I MSDs are restricted to boats 65 feet long or less and treat the sewage to specified standards before being discharged overboard. Type II MSDs are required for vessels greater than 65 feet and have higher treatment standards for the discharged effluent than Type I units. Type III MSDs prevent the overboard discharge of treated or untreated sewage by pumping it into a holding tank. U.S. Coast Guard approved Type I and II MSDs are identified with certification labels. No label is required for holding tanks that hold sewage at ambient temperatures and pressures.

Pumpout stations are used to empty holding tanks and toilet dump stations are available for portable toilets. Information on the availability of these locations varies considerably from state to state. In some cases locations are posted on websites. Some nautical almanacs, such as Reed's, include pumpout station locations. You can also check with your local U.S. Coast Guard District or state boating office for the latest information on pumpout station locations and no-discharge zones.

Portable toilets are often the choice for small powerboats. They can be easily carried on and off the boat.

Negligent Operation

Negligent or grossly negligent operation of a vessel that endangers lives and/or property is prohibited by law. Grossly negligent operation is a criminal offense and an operator may be fined up to $5,000, imprisoned for one year, or both. Examples that may constitute negligent or grossly negligent operation include:
• Operating a boat in a designated swimming area
• Operating a boat while under the influence of alcohol or drugs
• Excessive speed in the vicinity of other boats or in regulated waters
• Hazardous waterskiing or other water sports practices
• Bowriding or riding on the seatback, gunwale or transom.

A pumpout symbol identifies a pumpout station.

Speed Regulations

Boats must be operated within posted speed limits at all times. When no limits are posted, a boat must be operated at a speed so it will not endanger others. This includes proceeding at a speed below wake-producing speeds (below 5 mph) when passing marinas, docks with boats tied alongside, restricted anchorages and swimming areas. You are responsible for any damage caused by the wake of your boat. Navigation Rule 6 defines *safe speed* as a speed that will allow a vessel to take proper and effective action to avoid collision and be stopped within a distance appropriate to the prevailing circumstances and conditions.

Termination of Use Act

This act gives the Coast Guard the authority to board a vessel at any time. If an unsafe condition is found, the boat operator must follow the directions of the Coast Guard Boarding Officer to take immediate steps necessary for the safety of those aboard. These steps may include direction to (a) correct the unsafe condition immediately; (b) proceed to a mooring, dock, or anchorage; or (c) suspend further use of the boat until the condition is corrected.

For the purpose of the Act, "unsafe condition" includes:
• insufficient number of Coast Guard approved life jackets
• improper display of navigation lights
• insufficient fire extinguishers
• an overloaded boat
• fuel leakage or fuel in bilges
• improper ventilation of fuel tanks and engine spaces
• improper backfire flame control
• an obvious unsafe situation

Boating Accidents

Accident Reporting
Immediate notification is required if a person dies or disappears as a result of a recreational boating accident. The following notification should be provided to the nearest state boating authority.
• *Date, time and location of the accident*
• *Name of each person who died or disappeared*
• *Number and name of the vessel*
• *Name and address of the owner and the operator*

The highest incidents of accidents occur in good weather, in the mid-to-late afternoon and during peak boating periods. Most non-fatal boating accidents result from collisions with other boats, but predominance of fatalities occur because of capsizing and falling overboard.

A formal accident report must be submitted within 48 hours if a person dies or disappears or there are injuries requiring more than first aid. A formal report must be submitted within ten days for accidents involving more than $2,000.00 damage or the complete loss of a vessel. Accident report forms may be obtained at any office where boats are registered. State requirements for reporting boating accidents may be more stringent than federal requirements. Check with local marine patrol or the state Boating Law Administrator.

Alcohol Abuse. Boating accident statistics continue to show a high correlation between boating fatalities and alcohol use. Even in small amounts, ingestion of alcohol impairs vision, coordination, balance, awareness and judgment, and increases effects of sun and fatigue. It also hastens the body's heat loss thus shortening survival time in the water.

Because of alcohol-related boating accidents, most states have enacted "operating under the influence" laws. A blood alcohol content of 0.08 (0.10 in some states) or greater constitutes being legally intoxicated. Most of these laws also allow an officer to make a determination of intoxication based on observation of an operator's behavior. Refusal to submit to toxicological testing is automatic presumption of intoxication.

Rendering Assistance. A person in charge of a vessel is required by the Navigation Rules to assist any individual in danger at sea if it can be done without seriously endangering the vessel or those on board. Failure to render assistance will result in a fine of up to $1,000 or imprisonment up to two years. A person rendering assistance in good faith to others who do not object is not liable for damages if he or she acts reasonably and prudently.

Safety & Security Zones

These zones were established to prevent attacks on U.S. Naval vessels, commercial ships, and critical infrastructure. You should not operate your boat near military vessels, cruise ships, commercial ships, commercial port operations, power plants, and facilities for military and petroleum operations. Additionally, you should not stop or anchor under bridges or in shipping channels. Violations of these zones could result in legal action or injury.

Naval Vessel Protection Zone. This zone has specific restrictions. You must not approach within 100 yards of any U.S. Naval vessel, and you must operate at minimum speed within 500 yards. If you need to pass within 100 yards to ensure a safe passage in accordance with the Navigation Rules, you must contact the U.S. Naval vessel or the U.S. Coast Guard escort vessel on VHF radio (Channel 16) for authorization. Violations of the Naval Vessel Protection Zone are a felony offense, punishable by up to 6 years in prison and/or up to $250,000 in fines.

Diving Operations

Under Inland and International Navigation Rules, a vessel engaged in diving operations during the day may display a rigid replica of International Code Flag ALFA not less than 3.3 feet (1 meter) in height. This display is exhibited only by the vessel engaged in diving operations and signifies its inability to maneuver in accordance with the rules. It carries with it no special separation or maneuvering requirements for other boats other than to keep out of the way of the diving vessel.

International Code Flag ALFA (represents the letter, "A")

The Sport Divers flag has no official status in federal regulations. It is recognized by the Coast Guard as a flag indicating diving operations and, unlike the ALFA flag, it is used to mark the locations of divers in the water. Many states have enacted regulations requiring the display of the Sport Divers flag and specify standoff distances as well. A minimum of 100 feet is recommended but divers frequently stray considerable distances from their marker and separations of up to 300 feet are recommended in open waters. Like flag ALFA, the Sport Divers flag should be of rigid construction and conspicuously displayed. An operator of a vessel conducting diving operations should only display this flag to mark the site of diving operations. Having it painted on the topsides of a boat or flying the flag while proceeding out an inlet at 15 plus knots dilutes the meaning of the flag and has led to unintentional abuse by passing boaters.

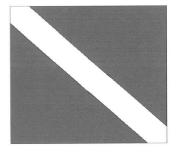

Sport Divers Flag

Prevention of Boat and Equipment Theft

Theft of boats and equipment can be a concern. Some of this can be prevented by the following steps:

- Mark your Hull Identification Number (HIN) in a hidden location on your boat. On boats without HINs, it is often possible to "clear fiberglass" over a duplicate of the boat's registration number on the interior of the hull.
- Mark or engrave all valuable equipment with an identification number.
- Keep valuables out of sight.
- Remove valuable equipment, including keys and certificate of number (registration) when you are away from your boat. Have a convenient boat "pack-up" kit that you take with you to your boat that contains all these items.
- Lock your boat and trailer to some immovable object such as a fence or a tree. For long-term storage consider removing trailer tires.
- Use a trailer hitch lock.
- Remove small outboard motors when not in use or lock them to the transom with a lock and chain.

REVIEW QUESTIONS

1. A wearable type of life jacket that is not designed to turn an unconscious person over from a face down position to a vertical or slightly backward position is a _____.
   a. Type I
   b. Type III
   c. Type IV

2. All boats operating in U.S. coastal waters, the Great Lakes, territorial seas and those waters connected directly to them up to a point where they narrow to less than _____ are required to carry U.S. Coast Guard approved visual distress signals.
   a. 2 miles
   b. 5 miles
   c. 10 miles

3. The minimum number of hand portable fire extinguishers required on a recreational boat is based on the _____ of the boat.

4. A person in charge of a vessel is required by law to provide assistance to any individual in danger at sea if it can be done without seriously _____ the vessel or those on board.

5. A red flag with a diagonal white stripe is called the _____.

Answers: 1) b. Type III 2) a. 2 miles 3) overall length 4) endangering 5) Sport Divers flag

11. On-Board Systems

KEY CONCEPTS
- ▶ Electrical systems
- ▶ Marine VHF/DSC radio
- ▶ Bilge systems
- ▶ Marine Sanitation Devices (MSDs)
- ▶ Fresh water systems
- ▶ Stoves

This chapter covers the basics of essential systems you will encounter on board most powerboats, but we suggest you also read and study manufacturers' manuals for more complete information on the specific systems used on your boat.

Electrical Systems

Most powerboats use a 12-volt DC electrical system. In smaller outboards, there is generally one 12-volt battery used for both starting and supporting other electrical systems, while larger boats may have a battery (or batteries) dedicated to starting the engine and another battery (or set of batteries) used to power lights, instruments, pumps and other equipment. On boats with multiple battery sources, a battery switch allows you to select the different battery systems. Whenever you start an engine or turn on lights or other equipment, you drain power from the batteries. The alternator on the engine charges the batteries when the engine is running, similar to the method used with a car. Larger powerboats may have a shore power outlet that enables you to plug into shore power to charge your batteries. If you have this type of outlet, your boat requires a battery charger to convert the AC (alternating current) shore power into DC (direct current) power.

Battery switch allows management of multiple batteries.

Most battery switches have four positions: #1 (battery one), #2 (battery two), ALL (turns on both battery systems), and OFF (shuts off all batteries). To start the engine, set the battery switch to the "start" position (either 1 or 2). If the starting battery's charge is too low to turn over the engine, first switch to the other battery, and if that doesn't work, try ALL (both).

Shore power outlets provide electricity for charging batteries, if the boat's electrical system has a battery charger.

Larger cruising powerboats may also have a 110-volt AC electrical system to operate AC lights and appliances such as hair dryers, coffee makers, blenders, TVs, heaters and electric tools. To use the AC fixtures and appliances, you will either need to be plugged into shore power or have a method of generating AC power on board. This can be done by an AC generator (genset) or by an inverter, which transforms DC battery power to AC.

Battery Tips

- *Keep your batteries charged.*
- *Turn off electrical fixtures and equipment when not in use.*
- *Leave battery switches in the OFF position when leaving your boat (your automatic bilge pump should be wired separately).*
- *Don't reposition the battery switch with the engine running without first checking the electrical system manual to see whether this can cause a problem.*

Battery Inspection

- Batteries and their boxes are secured and should always have a cover to avoid shorting the terminals inadvertently.
- Batteries should not be located in a confined space where accumulated battery gases may be exposed to an electrical spark and cause an explosion.
- Make sure battery terminals have no corrosion and cables are securely attached.
- Check the fluid levels of the batteries, if possible.
- Insulation on electrical wires is in good condition with no cracks or worn spots.

Marine VHF/DSC Radio

The marine VHF radiotelephone system is a line of sight, Very High Frequency system and provides local marine weather forecasts, two-way voice communication with nearby boats and marinas and access to emergency assistance. The VHF radio is limited by horizon, typically 10 to 15 miles for ship-to-ship communication and 20 to 30 miles for ship to shore, depending on the height of the antennas. At the low-power setting, these ranges are reduced. Handheld VHF radios typically have ranges of only a few miles.

Digital Selective Calling (DSC). DSC allows boaters to send or receive distress, urgency, safety and routine radiotelephone calls to or from any similarly equipped vessel or shore station, without requiring either party to be near a radio loudspeaker. With DSC, you can "direct dial" and "ring" other radios, or allow others to "ring" you. Users of a VHF/DSC radio must obtain a Maritime Mobile Service Identity (MMSI) number which is available from BoatUS, the FCC, Sea Tow, or the United States Power Squadrons. When the Distress button is activated, an automatically formatted distress alert will be instantly sent to the U.S. Coast Guard and any DSC radio within range. This alert will send the following information: your MMSI number, latitude and longitude position (radio must be connected to a GPS), and the nature of distress if entered. The U.S. Coast Guard's response to your distress alert will automatically switch your radio to Channel 16 for voice communication.

ONLINE...DSC: http://www.navcen.uscg.gov/

Channel Designations. Each channel is authorized for a specific purpose. Check your nautical almanac or go to www.navcen.uscg.gov for a complete list of channel designations. The channels of greatest interest to the recreational boater are:

Channel	Purpose
1, 2, 3, 4 – Weather	Provide continuous local marine weather forecasts, including storm warnings and watches.
9 – Boater Calling	Is a supplementary calling channel for recreational boaters to relieve congestion on Channel 16. It is NOT an emergency channel. In FL, GA and SC, it is used for bridge openings.
13, 67 – Navigation Safety	Used to communicate navigational information between vessels, such as meeting and passing situations. Vessels greater than 65 feet long maintain a listening watch on Channel 13 in U.S. waters (67 for lower Mississippi River). Channel 13 is also used at most locks and drawbridges.
16 – Distress, Safety & Calling	Used in emergencies, or to get attention for calling another station. Except in an emergency, upon receiving a response, advise the other boat to switch to a non-commercial channel. Routine radio checks are prohibited on this channel.
22A – U.S. Coast Guard Liaison and Maritime Safety Information Broadcasts	Is the principal channel for communication with the Coast Guard, except for distress and safety calls on Channel 16. It is monitored constantly and is the source for marine information broadcasts. To use Channel 22A, set VHF radio to the U.S. setting.
68, 69, 71 & 78 – Non-Commercial	Used for "intership" (boat to boat) and "ship to shore" communication for recreational boaters. Switch to one of these channels after initiating on Channel 16 (or 9).
70 – Digital Selective Calling	Restricted to Digital Selective Calling (DSC) communication.
72 – Non-Commercial	Restricted to only "intership" communication for recreational boaters.

Fixed mount VHF radios use the boat's battery for power and are required to have DSC if made after 1999. Adjust the squelch control by turning it down just under the crackling sound.

Most handheld VHF radios do not have DSC with GPS capability, but this one does. Note display of the latitude/longitude position.

Radio Communication Basics

- The high/low power switch on a VHF radio allows the user to select a power transmitter setting. Most communications should be attempted on the low power setting and only switched to high if needed.
- Use only those channels identified for recreational boating.
- Radio communication is public and shared. Speak clearly, be brief, and don't use profanity.
- Any vessel calling in an emergency always has priority.
- When making an "intership" (boat to boat) call:
  1. Initiate the call on Channel 16, or 9 if it is the designated calling channel for your area. Note: DSC Channel 70 may be used for "intership" when MMSI of vessel being called is known.
  2. Identify the boat you're calling, then identify your boat by saying "This is" followed by your boat's name. EXAMPLE: "Resolute, Resolute, Resolute. This is Sabino. Over." "Over" indicates this is the end of my transmission and a response is desired.
  3. Once contact is made, you must switch to a non-commercial channel, if both of you are recreational boaters.

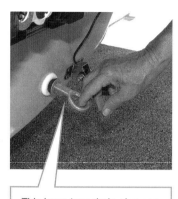

This lever-type drain plug can be easily removed to drain the bilge and secured in place to prevent loosening from vibration.

Electric bilge pumps (A) can be automatically activated by a float switch (B).

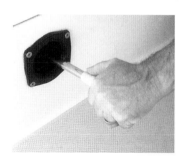

Smaller powerboats often have manual bilge pumps.

- The procedures for calling a shore station are the same, except if the shore station has an assigned operating channel, call them on that frequency instead of Channel 16 or 9.
- When ending a call:
  1. Each boat must give its name followed by the word "Out." "Out" indicates this is the end of my transmission and no response is desired or required. Do not use "over" or "over and out." EXAMPLE: "This is Resolute. Out." and "Sabino. Out."
  2. Both boats switch back to Channel 16.
- DSC Distress alerts or "MAYDAY" distress calls are made when a vessel or person is threatened by grave and imminent danger requiring immediate assistance. To send a DSC Distress alert, push and hold the Distress button until a "beep" is heard (don't push it more than once). When the Coast Guard receives your distress call your VHF automatically switches to Channel 16, and you should be prepared to answer their questions about your situation. To make a "MAYDAY" distress call, repeat "MAYDAY" three times followed by "This is" and repeat your boat's name three times. EXAMPLE: "MAYDAY, MAYDAY, MAYDAY. This is Lead Balloon, Lead Balloon, Lead Balloon." This is followed by your distress message — remember the three Ws: WHO you are, WHERE you are, and WHAT is your type of distress, assistance desired, and any other information to help with the rescue. EXAMPLE: "MAYDAY. This is Lead Balloon. We are one nautical mile east of Cape May. We are on fire and sinking. Two people are severely injured. Request immediate assistance. There are a total of five people on board. Boat is a 40-foot powerboat with white deck and topsides. Sending up red parachute flares and activating EPIRB. Over."
- "PAN-PAN" (pahn-pahn) urgency calls are made when there is a very urgent message concerning the safety (but is not life-threatening) of a vessel or some person on board or within sight. Use "PAN-PAN, PAN-PAN, PAN-PAN" instead of "MAYDAY, MAYDAY, MAYDAY."
- "SECURITE" (see-cur-ee-tay) calls are used to send a message concerning the safety of navigation or giving important meteorological warnings. SECURITE is spoken three times.

Bilge Systems

The bilge is located along the inside bottom of a boat where water from leaks, rain, waves or washdowns may collect. Many powerboats have a drainage system that allows you to drain either the entire bilge or various compartments in the bilge through drain holes in the transom when the boat is hauled out of the water. These are closed with drain plugs, which are either screwed in or locked in place by expanding the plug using a lever. *Make sure these plugs are secured before launching your boat.*

Boats that have a battery system for lights and electrical equipment usually have an electric bilge pump. These pumps often have a float switch that automatically turns on the pump when water in the bilge reaches a certain level, or they can be manually activated. Boats with electric pumps also carry manual pumps for emergencies.

There are drainage systems on some small boats that allow bilge water to exit the stern when the boat is at planing speed. Boats with this system will have drain plugs accessible from inside the boat.

Bilge System Inspection
• Check the bilge regularly for water or oil. If there is any oil, it cannot be pumped overboard and must be collected for disposal ashore.
• Carry extra drain plugs.
• Stow manual bilge pumps or pump handles in a accessible location.
• Keep intake screens on bilge pumps free of debris.
• Make sure float switch on electric pump operates freely.

Marine Sanitation Devices (MSDs)

Marine toilets (heads) generally do not have the capacity of toilets in the home. They tolerate less toilet paper and NO foreign objects. Raw-water (seawater) is pumped into the toilet bowl and the discharge is pumped into a holding tank or treatment device. With an electrically operated toilet, a push button is used to flush it. Manually operated toilets have a hand or foot lever or a twist knob that is used to let water into the bowl while a pump handle is used to pump the water in and out of the bowl. Whatever toilet type is used, always make sure the raw-water seacock is open before using, and close the valves, seacock(s) and seat lid when finished.

Electrically operated heads use a push-button to flush.

Manual heads may have a foot lever instead of a hand lever or twist knob. Depress the pedal to let water in and release it to stop.

Manual Head Operation Tips
• *Open raw-water seacock.*
• *Pump a small amount of water into the bowl before using.*
• *After flushing, pump additional strokes to make sure the discharge line is clear.*
• *Close seacock after use.*

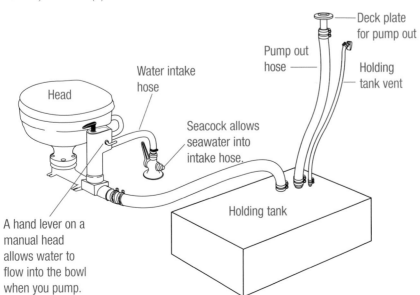

Deck plate for pump out

Pump out hose

Holding tank vent

Water intake hose

Head

Seacock allows seawater into intake hose.

Holding tank

A hand lever on a manual head allows water to flow into the bowl when you pump.

Larger boats often have a pressurized water system with "on/off" faucets (above) and may also have a manual pump water system (operated by black handle above) to conserve water. Some manual pumps are operated by pumping a foot lever (below). A foot pump lets you use both hands while pumping.

MSD Tips
- *Make sure all valves and seacock(s) are open before using.*
- *Stop pumping if you encounter resistance.*
- *Don't put anything in the head except a small amount of toilet paper or something that has been swallowed first.*
- *Close valves and seacock(s) after using.*
- *Leave area clean for the next person.*

Fresh Water System

Boats carry a limited amount of fresh water in one or several water tanks, depending on the size of the boat. As a result, water conservation is always a consideration, especially if you cannot conveniently refill tanks. To help conserve water, a manual water pressure system is typically used which you pump with your hand or foot to get water from a faucet. Larger powerboats with several tanks and a sufficient battery system usually have a pressurized system powered by an electric pump so that water comes out of a faucet whenever you turn it on.

Filling Fresh Water Tanks

❶ Close sink faucets so water doesn't run out when filling.
❷ Run the water hose for 30 seconds to clear debris before filling tanks.
❸ Check the deck fill plate to see it's labeled "water" before filling.
❹ After filling, tighten deck fill cap securely so water tank does not get contaminated.

Fresh Water Tips
- *Turn off pressure water switch when everyone is on deck or retired for the night, and when leaving the boat unattended.*
- *Close valves and faucets when not in use.*
- *If the pressure water pump is running constantly, check the faucets, system and tanks for leaks. If the pump runs continuously, it will burn out once the water tank is empty.*
- *Conserve water.*

Sumps

Drains from showers and iceboxes are usually below the surface of the outside seawater. They need to drain into a sump tank in the bilge that is emptied by a sump pump. If the tank is not pumped out and it fills up, water will not drain from the shower or icebox. The intake on the sump pump should be inspected and cleaned regularly to prevent it getting clogged by debris and hair. To avoid reverse flow in the discharge line due to siphoning, the line will frequently be looped above the seawater surface with an air breaker valve at the top of the loop or

There is usually a deck fill cap for each water tank. Be sure you fill the one marked "water," not "waste" or "fuel."

exit through the hull above the seawater. Keep the air breaker valve clean. If it gets clogged up, the discharge line may siphon seawater into the sump and flood the shower. Sinks are normally positioned higher than the seawater level and will usually drain directly overboard.

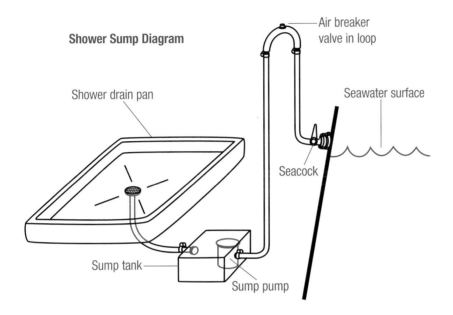

Shower Sump Diagram

Air breaker valve in loop

Shower drain pan

Seawater surface

Seacock

Sump tank

Sump pump

Stoves

Stoves on cruising powerboats come in several sizes and types. They can range from portable single-burner butane stoves and two-burner alcohol stoves (on smaller boats) to propane gas or electric stoves (on larger boats).

Alcohol Stoves. Alcohol stoves require preheating (priming) of the burner to make the pressurized fuel vaporize on contact and burn. When the burner is hot, the fuel can be turned on and ignited for cooking. Water will put out an alcohol fire.

❶ Pump the tank, then open the valve to run alcohol into burner cup.
❷ To prime the stove, close valve and ignite alcohol in burner cup.
❸ When the alcohol in the cup has burned out, open valve to the burner to access fuel. Ignite the vaporizing alcohol at the burner.
❹ When finished cooking, shut off valve and release pressure.

Alcohol stoves are popular for smaller boats.

Stove Safety Tips
- *Locate fire extinguishers.*
- *Shut off fuel when stove is not in use.*
- *Don't leave burner and oven controls on after you turn off the fuel supply.*
- *Don't forget to close the tank valves when leaving the boat.*

Propane stoves are efficient and convenient, but need to be used carefully. A solenoid switch (above) allows quick shutoff of propane tank.

Portable gas or charcoal grills are often used, but be considerate of others by not letting smoke or sparks from your barbecue drift downwind onto their boats.

Propane Stoves. Propane gas heated stoves are easy to use, but because propane is heavier than air it must be used with care. Leaking gas can settle in the bilge and could be ignited by a spark.

❶ Turn on the tank valve and then the solenoid switch.

❷ Strike the match or starter before turning on the burner control.

❸ When finished cooking, turn off the solenoid and then the burners. Check that all controls, including the oven, are off.

Propane Safety System

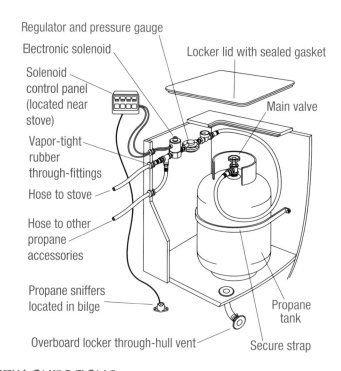

- Regulator and pressure gauge
- Electronic solenoid
- Solenoid control panel (located near stove)
- Vapor-tight rubber through-fittings
- Hose to stove
- Hose to other propane accessories
- Propane sniffers located in bilge
- Overboard locker through-hull vent
- Locker lid with sealed gasket
- Main valve
- Propane tank
- Secure strap

REVIEW QUESTIONS

1. The type of electrical system most powerboats use for starting, instruments, pumps and lights is a _____.
   a. 6-volt b. 9-volt c. 12-volt
2. Except for distress and safety calls, when contacting the U.S. Coast Guard on a marine VHF radio, the preferred channel to use is _____.
   a. 16 b. 22A c. 71
3. When a person or vessel is in grave and imminent danger, the VHF distress call is preceded by the word _____ spoken three times.
4. Before using a manual or electrical pump on a marine toilet, make sure the raw-water _____ is open.
5. Propane gas must be handled with care because it is _____ than air and can settle in the bilge.

Answers: 1) c. 12-volt 2) b. 22A 3) Mayday 4) seacock 5) heavier

12. The Environment

KEY CONCEPTS
- ► Weather
- ► Thunderstorms
- ► Winds
- ► Tides & currents

Weather, tides and currents play an important role in the success and enjoyment of a trip or a day's outing. Current weather conditions and forecasts are found in newspapers, on the radio, television, Internet, and weather applications can be downloaded onto your mobile phone. Get in the habit of keeping track of the weather to get a picture of upcoming weather. While on the water be constantly aware of what is happening in the sky and periodically check weather broadcasts on your VHF radio or mobile phone.

A weather chart downloaded to a mobile phone.

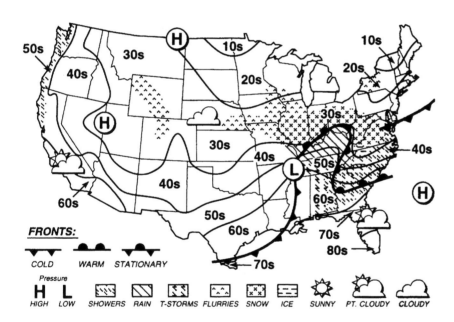

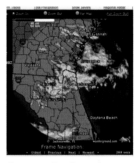

An example of a radar image from a mobile phone.

This newspaper weather map shows high and low pressure systems, fronts, types of precipitation, sky conditions, and temperatures.

Weather

North American weather systems generally move from west to east. The speed at which these systems move depends on many factors. These include their strength, the location of the jet stream and the time of year. Typically, weather a couple of hundred miles to the west of you can be your weather for tomorrow.

High pressure system (H) usually indicates dry, sunny weather with cooler air and lighter winds than low pressure systems.

Barometers help predict weather by measuring atmospheric pressure. Usually, a rising barometer signals good weather; a falling one warns of poor weather.

Wispy, thin cirrus clouds often mean good weather for the day, but also predict an approaching change in the weather.

White, puffy cumulus clouds are often an indicator of good weather, and are typically seen after a cold front has passed through.

Towering cumulonimbus clouds, or thunderheads, are usually accompanied by heavy rain, strong winds and lightning.

Bays and harbors can be shrouded in fog when warm, moist air from the land meets cold water and cools below its dew point.

Low pressure system (L) is usually accompanied by a warm or cold front and inclement weather with stronger winds, rain and sometimes storms.

A front develops when colder, dry air meets warmer, moist air.

Warm fronts occur when lighter, warmer air rides up over heavier, cooler air. This front usually moves more slowly (about half the speed) than a cold front and brings overcast skies, rain and bad weather with the possibility of thunderstorms and strong winds. High cirrus clouds are first seen as the front approaches. After a warm front has passed, the air will be warmer.

Cold fronts occur when heavier, cooler air pushes under lighter, warmer air. It moves rapidly and is often accompanied by towering cumulus or cumulonimbus clouds, rain, strong winds and possible thunderstorms. After a cold front has passed, the air will be cooler. Tip: the symbol for a cold front can be remembered as icicles on a wire.

Observation	Prediction
Sun and clear sky in the morning	Onshore winds during the day, and offshore winds (land breezes) during the night usually dying in the morning.
Thermal sea breeze	Increasing strength during the day as the land heats up and decreasing or dying at night as the land cools. Expect the wind to veer clockwise as velocity increases. In some parts of the country, increasing sea breezes will be accompanied by growing cumulus clouds.
Calm, overcast days	Continued calm and overcast, unless the sun comes out.
Cold and warm fronts	Showers or rain, changing air temperature, winds shifting in a clockwise direction. Cold fronts usually move faster than warm fronts.
High cirrus clouds	A warm front with rain and changing winds should appear in a couple of days. Clouds will get lower and more dense as the front gets closer.
Cumulus clouds growing taller (cumulonimbus)	Thunderstorms and strong winds.
Dark clouds approaching	A squall or storm.

Personal Observation. Recognizing the patterns of weather systems and local conditions is an important part of your preparation and awareness on land and on the water. Be observant and learn to recognize the signals of impending weather from changes in wind direction, cloud patterns, air temperature and air pressure.

Thunderstorms. The familiar afternoon forecast of a 20% chance of thunderstorms can sound routine, but few weather phenomena can threaten boaters as quickly and as dramatically as a thunderstorm. They often advance on the heels of a sea breeze and if not detected early, can overtake you before you can reach safe haven. The first clue of their approach might be a distant, high altitude arc of cirrus clouds that often forms above cumulonimbus clouds. Any change in the color, shape or size of clouds means some change in weather is coming. The more pronounced the change, the more significant the weather. As a thunderstorm develops, the top part of the thunder-cloud becomes anvil-shaped and streams in the direction that the storm is moving. The wind ahead of a thunderstorm can be variable or steady, and may weaken and die as the storm approaches. When the roll cloud passes overhead, the wind will shift and blow violently with gusts that can exceed 50 knots. Heavy rain begins just behind the roll cloud.

A distant cumulonimbus cloud with a clearly visible anvil is probably going to pass to the side of you, but a rapidly growing cumulonimbus cloud with no visible anvil may be headed in your direction. Many storms develop erratic paths so their direction could suddenly change. The rough distance to a storm may be determined by timing the interval between a lightning flash and the associated thunderclap. Divide the time in seconds by five for the distance in statute miles.

Squalls often accompany cold fronts and bring strong winds. If you see a squall line developing, it's time to seek shelter.

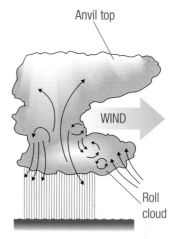

The anvil top of a thundercloud streams in the direction that the storm is moving.

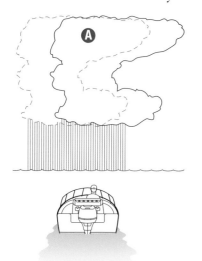

Both sides of cloud **A** are moving to the right of the boat, the storm should miss and pass to your right.

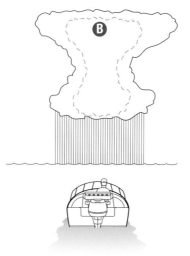

The left side of cloud **B** is moving to the left and the right side to the right, this indicates you are in its path.

Bad Weather Signals
- *Increase in cloud cover and darkening skies*
- *Sudden decrease or increase in wind velocity*
- *Change in wind direction*
- *Lightning nearby or in the distance*
- *Thunder in the distance*
- *Gusty wind conditions*

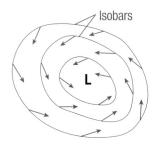

Isobars

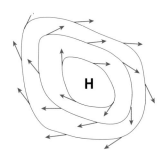

Wind spirals inward and counterclockwise around a low **L** generally following the concentric lines on the map called isobars. Tightly spaced isobars indicate strong winds.

Wind spirals outward and clockwise around a high **H**.

Winds

Winds are created from pressure differences in the atmosphere, blowing from higher toward lower pressure. Winds can be generated by major weather systems or local conditions.

Winds Around a High Pressure System. In a high pressure system, the pressure increases as you move toward its center, which will cause air to blow outward from the center. However, the turning of the earth causes this air to spiral out in a clockwise direction in the northern hemisphere.

Winds Around a Low Pressure System. In a low pressure system, the pressure decreases as you move toward its center, which will cause air to blow inward toward the center. The rotation of the earth will make this air spiral inward in a counterclockwise direction in the northern hemisphere.

Onshore and Offshore Winds. Local winds can be caused by the differences in air temperature over land and water. Sea breezes are formed as warm air rises above the land, drawing in cooler air from over the water. As the land heats up in the afternoon, the velocity of these winds will increase. Local offshore winds often occur at night or in the morning when the land has cooled and the warmer air over the water rises, drawing cooler air from over the land.

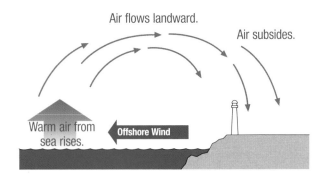

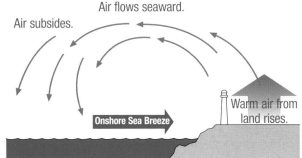

Topographic Effects on Winds. Wind direction and strength can be affected by local topography. For instance, on rivers surrounded by elevated land, the wind will tend to funnel down or up the river, following bends in the river.

Tides

Tides are the vertical movement of water and are caused primarily by the gravitational pull of the moon on the earth with the sun's pull a secondary factor. As the moon rotates around the earth, its gravitational force "pulls" the earth's water toward it. As the moon moves, so does the water level in most bodies of ocean water. Typically, there are two high and two low tides each day on the east and west coasts of the U.S. In the Gulf of Mexico, tides vary between two highs and two lows a day to one high and one low a day with very unequal tides in between. With a watch, a tide table and a chart you can determine the depth of the water in which you are motoring or anchoring at any given time.

A tide table gives daily information regarding the times of high and low tides and their heights. The heights from the tide table are added (unless they are shown as a negative figure) to the depth shown on the nautical chart to determine the actual water depth at a particular location at high or low tide. Be aware that weather conditions can alter these predictions.

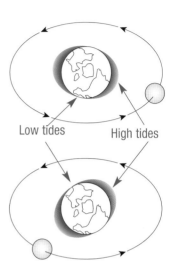

Low tides   High tides

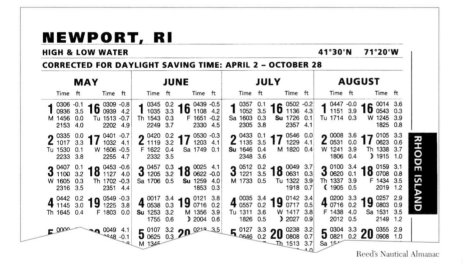

Reed's Nautical Almanac

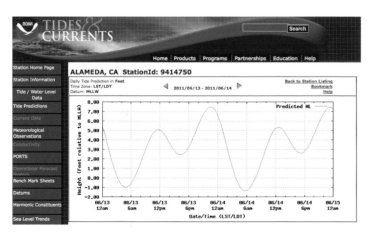

Graphical representations of the rise and fall of tides are available as well. Tables and charts of tides and currents can be downloaded from the Internet or as apps for your mobile phone, and are also available as printed publications in marine stores.

*ONLINE...*Tides:
http://tidesandcurrents.noaa.gov/tide_predictions.shtml
Current:
http://tidesandcurrents.noaa.gov/curr_pred.html

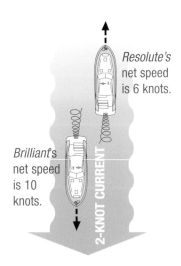

Resolute's net speed is 6 knots.

Brilliant's net speed is 10 knots.

2-KNOT CURRENT

This shows two powerboats motoring at 8 knots in a current of 2 knots. *Brilliant* has favorable current to increase its speed over the bottom (SOG) to 10 knots, while *Resolute* has to motor against the current, making only 6 knots of SOG.

Current table from the Internet

Currents

Current is the horizontal movement of water, and can be caused by a river's flow, tides, wind or ocean movements. The Gulf Stream off the U.S. East Coast is a well-known ocean current. In coastal areas, currents are caused by the tides falling and rising. Current affects all boats equally at any given instant. It can be compared to the situation where an adult and a small child are standing on a moving conveyor walkway, where both are moving at the same speed even though the adult is bigger and heavier. Traveling from one point to another, however, the effects of current on slow-moving boats is proportionately more than fast-moving boats because a slow-moving boat is exposed to the current for a greater length of time.

Tidal Current Table. These tables include times of maximum current and slack water (when tides change from ebb to flood or vice versa) as well as current velocity in knots (1 knot = 1 nautical mile per hour).

Tidal Current Chart. For some areas, current information may also be presented graphically. These are published in sets of 12, relating to the hours before or after high water or slack water. The arrows indicate current direction and the numbers indicate current velocity in knots. *Flood* is incoming current and *ebb* is outgoing current.

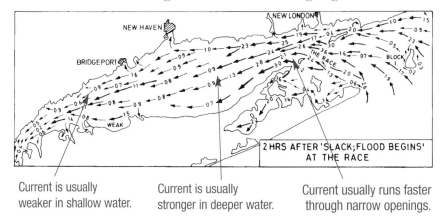

Current is usually weaker in shallow water.

Current is usually stronger in deeper water.

Current usually runs faster through narrow openings.

REVIEW QUESTIONS

1. Weather generally moves from _____ to _____ in the U.S.
2. The top part of a thundercloud is an _____ shape and _____ in the direction that the storm is moving.
3. Winds rotate in a _____ direction around a low pressure system.
4. Sea breezes or onshore winds generally occur at what time of the day?
   a. morning b. afternoon c. night
5. Tides are the _____ movement of water and current is the _____ movement of water.

Answers: 1) west; east 2) anvil; streams 3) counterclockwise 4) b. afternoon 5) vertical; horizontal

13. Navigation Rules

KEY CONCEPTS
- ▶ Inland Navigation Rules
- ▶ International Navigation Rules
- ▶ Maintaining a lookout
- ▶ Safe speed
- ▶ Navigation (running) lights
- ▶ Meeting situations

The fundamental purpose of the Navigation Rules is to help vessels avoid collisions. There are two sets of Rules. The *Inland Rules* apply to the navigable inland waters of the United States. These include the U.S. waters of the Great Lakes, harbors, rivers, bays and sounds on the shoreward side of the demarcation line, which defines the boundary between inland and international waters. The *International Rules* apply to the high seas and are known as the International Regulations for Preventing Collisions at Sea, 1972, abbreviated as 72 COLREGS. While the two sets of Rules are mostly similar, there are some notable differences in light and sound signals and situations in narrow channels. The *Navigation Rules, International-Inland* is available online, at some marine stores, or can be ordered from the U.S. Government Printing Office.

ONLINE... Online bookstore of U.S. Govt. Printing Office: http://bookstore.gpo.gov/
For *Navigation Rules, Intl.-Inland*: http://www.uscg.mil/vtm/navrules/navrules.pdf

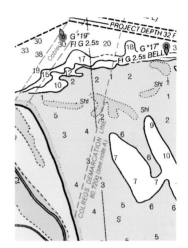

A magenta colored demarcation line depicts the boundary where Navigation Rules change from Inland Rules to International (72 COLREGS) Rules.

Maintaining a Proper Lookout. A vessel shall at all times maintain a proper lookout by sight and hearing and any other means available.

Safe Speed. A vessel shall at all times operate at a safe speed so that proper and effective action can be taken to avoid a collision or to stop within an appropriate distance. Safe speed is determined by visibility, traffic density, the boat's maneuverability, navigational hazards, water depth, wind, current and sea conditions.

Operating in Narrow Channels. A boat shall keep as near to the starboard (right) edge of a channel as possible. In shipping channels with adequate water depth outside the channel, a small powerboat should operate alongside the channel. A powerboat less than 66 feet long (20 meters) or a sailboat shall not impede passage of a vessel that can only operate in the channel. Do not anchor in a channel.

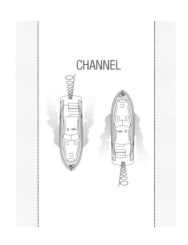

CHANNEL

The Inland Rules require that in narrow channels or fairways on the Great Lakes and Western Rivers, a vessel under power proceeding downbound with a following current shall have right-of-way over an upbound vessel heading against the current. The downbound vessel shall indicate manner and place of passing with appropriate sound signals.

Sound Signals

• A short blast is about one second's duration.

— A prolonged blast is from four to six seconds' duration.

For vessels in sight of each other:

• One short blast indicates *altering* course to starboard (International), or *intending* to alter course to starboard (Inland) when meeting or crossing.

• • Two short blasts indicate *altering* course to port (International), or *intending* to alter course to port (Inland) when meeting or crossing.

• • • Three short blasts indicate engine is in reverse (although vessel may still be moving forward).

• • • • • Five short blasts = danger.

Other sound signals:

— One prolonged blast is sounded by a vessel nearing a blind bend of a channel or fairway, or when departing a berth.

For other sound signals consult the *Navigation Rules, International-Inland.*

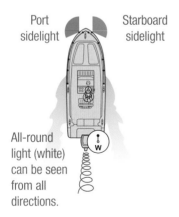

Port sidelight   Starboard sidelight

All-round light (white) can be seen from all directions.

Light requirement for a powerboat underway whose length is less than 39.4 feet (12 meters).

Sound Signals. Boats may provide information to other boats about their maneuvers through the use of sound signals. Nowadays, vessels may also use radio communication to make passing arrangements. This reduces the confusion generated by traditional sound signals in heavy traffic where it may be unclear who is being hailed. Monitoring radio communication is also an excellent way to gain awareness of vessel traffic. See Chapter 11 for information on channel designations of a marine VHF radio and their use.

Lights for Nighttime Operation. The Navigation Rules require "running" lights when operating from sunset to sunrise, during hours of restricted visibility or whenever it is deemed necessary. These lights can take many forms, such as sidelights, sternlights, masthead lights, all-round lights and towing lights. Their location and required visibility depend on the type and size of vessel. Some typical light arrangements are shown on pages 108-110. Refer to the Navigation Rules for additional light requirements for sailboats, Great Lakes vessels and vessels towing, pushing, fishing or restricted in their ability to maneuver.

Risk of Collision. Every vessel shall use all available means to determine if a risk of collision exists. If there is any doubt, it shall be assumed that a risk exists. To determine whether a risk exists, take a bearing of the other boat with your compass or by lining it up with a point on your boat. If the bearing remains unchanged, a collision will occur unless there is a change in course or speed. With large vessels or a tow at close range, a risk of collision may exist even when there is an appreciable change of bearing.

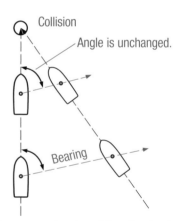

Collision

Angle is unchanged.

Bearing

If a compass bearing of the other boat remains constant and the distance between the boats is decreasing, you're on a collision course.

Meeting Situations. A boat that is required to keep out of the way of another vessel is the give-way vessel. It shall alter its course in ample time and with an obvious change of course and/or speed to signal that the rule is understood and action is being taken. The other vessel is the stand-on vessel and should maintain consistent course and speed. However, it is every vessel's obligation to avoid a collision. If it becomes apparent that the give-way vessel is not maneuvering in time to avoid a collision, a stand-on vessel should then change course and speed.

When vessels are approaching in sight of each other, the Rules for the following situations apply: crossing, head-on, overtaking, and responsibilities between vessels.

Crossing Situation Rule. When two powerboats are on an intersecting course, the boat on your starboard (right) side is the stand-on vessel, and the give-way vessel must alter course. Whenever possible, the give-way vessel should alter course to pass *astern* (behind) of the stand-on vessel.

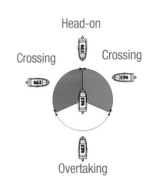

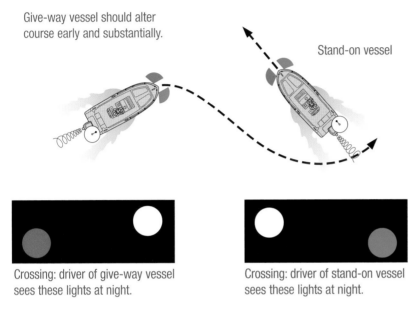

Give-way vessel should alter course early and substantially.

Stand-on vessel

Crossing: driver of give-way vessel sees these lights at night.

Crossing: driver of stand-on vessel sees these lights at night.

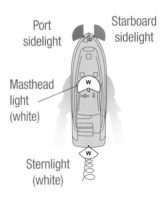

Port sidelight

Starboard sidelight

Masthead light (white)

Sternlight (white)

Light requirement for a powerboat (or sailboat using an engine) underway whose length is less than 164 feet (50 meters).

Tip: To quickly determine which boat must give way remember the colors of the port (red) and starboard (green) sidelights. If you see the red side of the other boat, think of it as a red traffic light signaling stop (or change course). If you see the green side, it's the same as a green light meaning go - maintain your speed and course.

Head-On Situation Rule. When two powerboats approach each other, they should alter course to starboard (right) so that they pass port (left) side to port side and signal with one short blast. If there is any doubt as to whether such a situation exists, it shall be assumed to exist. If you alter to port and pass starboard side to starboard side, the signal and response is two short blasts.

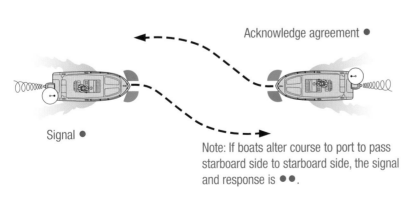

Acknowledge agreement ●

Signal ●

Note: If boats alter course to port to pass starboard side to starboard side, the signal and response is ● ●.

Head-on: drivers of both boats see these lights at night.

Overtaking: driver of give-way vessel sees this light at night.

Overtaking: driver of stand-on vessel sees these lights behind him.

Overtaking Situation Rule. The passing (overtaking) boat is the give-way vessel and may pass to either side of the stand-on vessel. A vessel is overtaking when it is in the area defined by the 135-degree arc of the other vessel's sternlight.

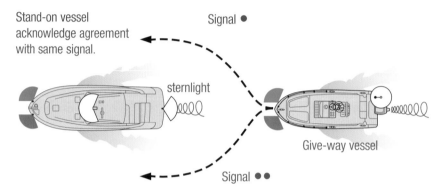

Stand-on vessel acknowledge agreement with same signal.

Signal ●

sternlight

Give-way vessel

Signal ● ●

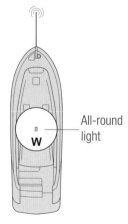

Light requirement for a boat being rowed or paddled: a flashlight is turned on in sufficient time to prevent a collision.

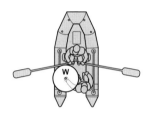

All-round light

Light requirement for an anchored boat less than 164 feet (50 meters). During the day, a black anchor ball is displayed. These requirements do not apply for boats less than 23 feet anchored away from a narrow channel, fairway, anchorage, or an area where vessels normally navigate.

Meeting Situations When In Restricted Visibility. Restricted visibility can be caused by fog, mist, falling snow, heavy rainstorms, or sandstorms. In conditions where boats cannot see one another, a distinct set of Rules exist.

• Maintain a careful lookout.

• Operate at a safe speed for the condition and be ready to maneuver immediately. A rule of thumb is to travel at a speed at which your boat can be stopped within half the distance of the prevailing visibility.

• Listen for sound signals. If you hear a fog signal from another vessel forward of your boat's beam, you shall slow down to minimum control speed and be prepared to stop until danger of collision is over.

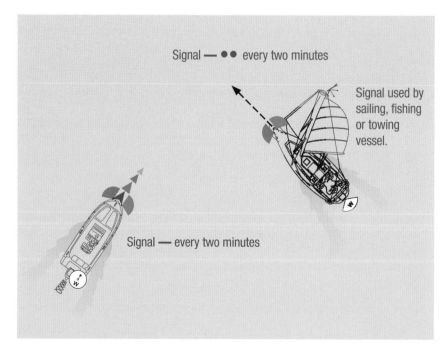

Signal — ● ● every two minutes

Signal used by sailing, fishing or towing vessel.

Signal — every two minutes

Traffic Separation Schemes. Areas with a high volume of shipping will often have traffic separation schemes, or vessel traffic lanes, that are reserved for use by large vessels and those with restricted maneuverability. You should stay clear of these schemes.

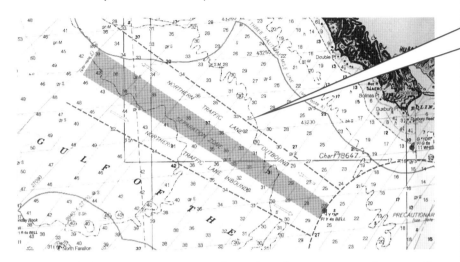

Responsibilities Between Vessels Rule. There are several types of vessels of which a powerboat underway shall keep clear. These are:
• a vessel not under command. Examples: a vessel on fire or one whose engines won't operate.
• a vessel which by the nature of its work is restricted in its ability to maneuver. Examples: a vessel dredging, or servicing a navigation mark or underwater cable.
• a vessel engaged in fishing with nets, lines or trawls that restrict its ability to maneuver. It does not include fishing with trolling lines.
• a boat using only a sail(s) for propulsion unless the sailboat is overtaking the powerboat.

REVIEW QUESTIONS

1. The fundamental purpose of the Navigation Rules is to help vessels avoid _____.
2. The boundary between inland and international waters is marked by a _____ line which is shown on _____.
3. If you are in a crossing situation, the boat on your _____ side is the give-way vessel.
4. When the bearing of an approaching boat does not change and its distance is decreasing, you are on a _____ course.
   a. separation b. safe c. collision
5. In restricted visibility, you should proceed at a speed that the boat can be stopped within _____ the distance of the visibility.
   a. quarter b. half c. twice

Answers: 1) collisions 2) demarcation: charts 3) port 4) c. collision 5) b. half

---

Your duties in a Traffic Separation Scheme are as follows:
▶ You should keep well clear of Traffic Separation Schemes if convenient.
▶ If you need to join the traffic in a scheme, you should do so at the ends if this is reasonable.
▶ When crossing a scheme, you are obliged to cross at right angles to the traffic flow at your best speed.
▶ The separation zone must be crossed at right angles as well. Do not resume your course or run along inside it parallel to the traffic.
▶ You can go around the edge of a Traffic Separation Scheme without being subject to the above rules.

The navigation rules contained in this course book summarize basic navigation rules for which a boat operator is responsible on inland waterways. Additional and more in-depth rules apply regarding various types of waterways, such as International Waters and Western Rivers, and operation in relation to commercial vessels and other watercraft. It is the responsibility of a boat operator to know and follow all the navigation rules. In those states that Inland Rules do not apply, the equivalent International, Western Rivers or Great Lakes rule(s) may be substituted by the Course Provider. For a complete listing of the navigation rules, refer to the document *Navigation Rules, International – Inland*. For State specific navigation requirements, refer to the state laws where you intend to boat.

14. Basic Navigation & Piloting Concepts

Line of longitude   Line of latitude

Lines of longitude appear parallel on the chart, but they converge toward the poles (see globe).

Scale   Soundings in feet
Chart datum (WGS84)

Heights in feet

Title block includes chart datum, scale, and measurement units for soundings and heights. Date that the chart was issued along with any corrections are located in bottom left corner. Keep current charts on board and update them with *Local Notices to Mariners* changes.

KEY CONCEPTS

▶ Chart basics
▶ Position
▶ GPS & plotter definitions
▶ Measuring distance
▶ Distance, speed & time

▶ Direction & the compass
▶ Waypoints
▶ GPS, the chart & accuracy
▶ Aids to navigation

Think "navigating and piloting" and most boaters immediately imagine GPS screens and chart plotters because these are the most common sources of access to navigation data. The primary tools, however, are the paper chart and a good pair of eyes. GPS makes using both of these easier, and a plotter in the right hands can render the paper almost redundant, but the navigator has to assume electronics will fail. This chapter deals with the concepts needed to pilot safely in daylight. Chapter 15 shows how to use these in practice when all is well, and how to handle that awful moment when the screens go blank.

The Chart

There are two basic types of charts: paper charts and electronic charts. To use a paper chart all you need is vision and some simple instruments while electronic charts can only be operated through an electronic chart plotter.

Most nautical charts use a Mercator projection to transfer the image of Earth's spherical surface onto a flat piece of paper. The primary advantage of a Mercator chart is that lines of latitude and longitude form an easy-to-use rectangular grid, which allows courses to be drawn as a straight line from one place to another.

Paper charts typically show areas of water and adjacent portions of coastline together with information useful for navigation, such as navigation aids (i.e., beacons and buoys), underwater features and landmarks on shore. Symbols and abbreviations are frequently used to convey this information, many of which are largely self-explanatory, but NOS (National Ocean Service) Chart No. 1 is a helpful reference for any you don't find obvious. The title block contains a great deal of important information, including units of soundings (water depths) and heights of land elevations. On this chart soundings are in feet. Other charts may have them in fathoms (1 fathom = 6 feet), fathoms and feet, or meters. If fathoms are used, fathoms with a feet subscript may be used in shallower water. For example, a depth of 4 fathoms and 3 feet would be indicated as 4_3. If the soundings unit is in meters, the soundings will be indicated in meters and tenths of meters with the tenths shown as a subscript. Thus, 1.3 meters would be 1_3. Note also the depth contour lines. These are often picked out in colors, making them easy to spot at a glance. If your chart doesn't cover enough ground for the passage you want to make, you might change to one drawn to a larger scale. This will show a wider spread of coastline, but will have less detail, so for safe piloting, you'll probably need both.

ONLINE... for Chart No. 1: http://www.nauticalcharts.noaa.gov/mcd/chartno1.htm

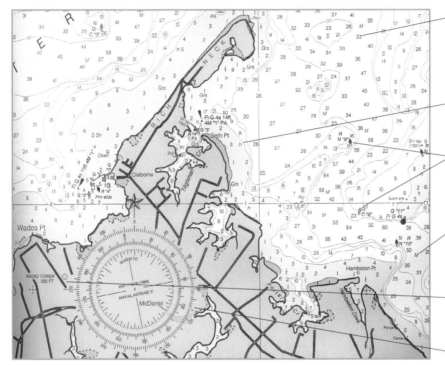

The small numbers scattered throughout the water are **soundings** or depths at low tide (at mean lower low water) at those particular points.

A **contour line** follows a constant water depth. Areas of shallower waters are indicated in light blue.

Symbols are used to indicate **aids to navigation**. Red and green diamond shapes indicate buoys (see page 121).

Types of bottom are indicated, such as mud, sand, grass or rocky that you can expect when looking for a place to anchor.

Onshore landmarks, such as towers, can be used as navigation references.

A **compass rose** is printed on every nautical chart.

Electronic charts do the same job as paper, but at first sight they are not as easy to read. This is because of scale. Charts used in plotters (other than PC plotters) come in various formats and are either preinstalled or bought separately on data cards and uploaded to the unit. Once installed into a plotter, they can be read.

Position of vessel

Course and speed over ground

Heading

Position of cursor

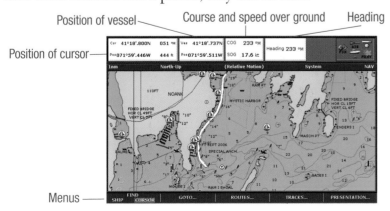

Menus

An electronic plotter screen showing a chart zoomed to a usable scale for general piloting.

GPS Settings

Check the default settings of your GPS and modify them to suit your needs. Here are some settings to consider.

- *Datum (WGS84 is standard, but must agree with the datum used for your chart)*
- *Speed (knots)*
- *Distance (nautical miles)*
- *Time (24-hour clock and local time)*
- *True or Magnetic North*
- *Latitude & Longitude (degrees, minutes, decimals of minutes)*

Any electronic chart contains all the information available within its boundaries, regardless of scale. If all this data were displayed, the chart would be unusable, so the plotter filters it for you. As you zoom in and out for an overview or more details, features appear and disappear. The plotter's default is often to center its view on your vessel, but if you need to see what's happening elsewhere you can move across the chart, then zoom in or out again. This method is the only way of using electronic charts. The more you do it, the easier it becomes, but the watchword is that unless you zoom right in, the chart may be hiding something vital.

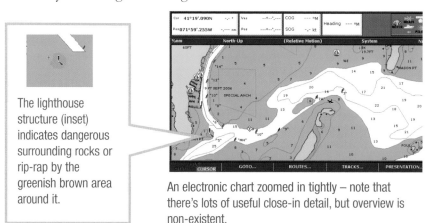

The lighthouse structure (inset) indicates dangerous surrounding rocks or rip-rap by the greenish brown area around it.

An electronic chart zoomed in tightly – note that there's lots of useful close-in detail, but overview is non-existent.

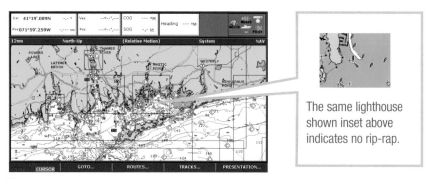

The same chart zoomed out for overview – note the lack of useful detail.

The same lighthouse shown inset above indicates no rip-rap.

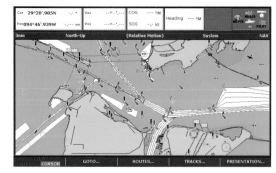

Plotters have menus full of tools but one of the easiest to access is often Declutter. This chart has been decluttered to clarify the overview. However, much vital detail is obscured.

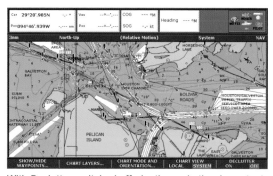

With Declutter switched off, depths and other important data are visible. It is critical never to leave a chart decluttered and to forget you have done so.

Position

Lines of latitude and longitude (lat/long) are used to define position on a chart. Both latitude and longitude are measured in degrees (°), minutes (') and decimals of minutes, or degrees, minutes and seconds ("). On a chart, minutes and seconds have nothing to do with time, they are simply subdivisions of a degree. 60 minutes equals 1 degree and 60 seconds equals 1 minute. Check to determine whether your chart is using decimals of minutes or seconds. Latitude is measured north or south from the Equator (0°) to the poles (90°) and longitude is measured east or west from Greenwich Observatory in England (0°) to the International Date Line in the Pacific Ocean (180°).

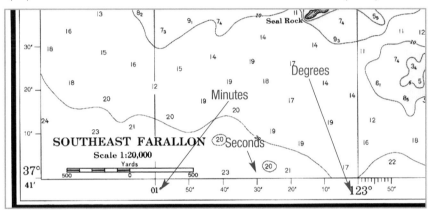

Plotting a Position on a Paper Chart

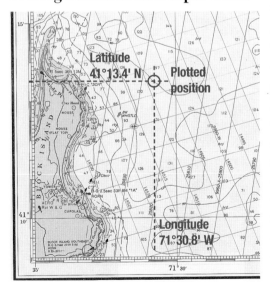

To plot a position of 41°13.4' North latitude and 71°30.8' West longitude (normally written or read out as 41 13.4N 71 30.8W), locate these positions on the latitude and longitude scales and transfer them by right-angles to the position on the chart. This can be done by any suitable instruments, including a chart protractor, dividers and parallel rulers.

Position on an Electronic Chart. Depending on how you have manipulated the menus, the position of your vessel or the plotter's cursor can generally be read off the data boxes in a chart plotter screen. This is because, with its built-in GPS locator, the plotter already knows the location of anything on the chart it is using.

SPEED	TRACK
0.0kt	**002**°T
LOCATION N 41°13.400' W 71°30.800'	ACCURACY **49**ft

GPS navigation screens vary, but the important thing when plotting is the position (location) of latitude and longitude.

Distance

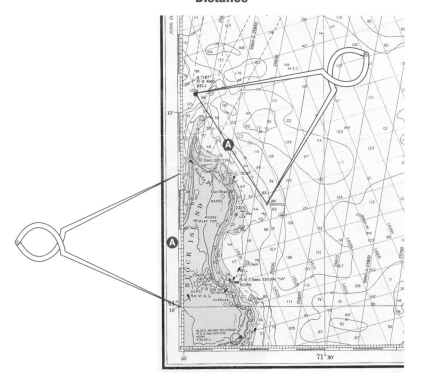

On the Paper Chart. One minute of latitude (NOT longitude) is equal to one nautical mile. This convenient arrangement means that to measure distance, you have only to define it **Ⓐ** on the chart with your dividers, then carry them over to the latitude scale near a latitude line where you've measured the distance and read off how many minutes and decimals of a minute their spread covers. In this case, the distance **Ⓐ** between the charted features is 3.4 miles (3.4 minutes of latitude).

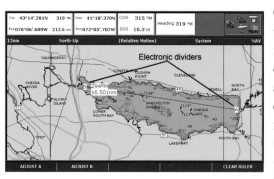

On the Plotter. If you search the menus, you'll find that many plotters have electronic dividers that do the same job as the real thing on a paper chart. This plotter calls them a ruler. Note the distance (16.501 nm) and bearing (294° M) readout on the line from A to B. Often, the distance you really want is how far something is from the yacht. This is readily measured on all plotters by placing the cursor on the object. The distance is then read off the cursor data box (top left-hand corner in this case).

Speed and Time

Having discovered how far it is from where you are to where you want to go, you'll probably want to know how long the trip will take, and how much fuel you may use. Because marine fuel consumption is generally measured in gallons per hour, rather than miles per gallon, you'll have to compare distance with time and speed as well. Speed at sea is measured in knots, which are nautical miles per hour (1 knot = 1.15 mph).

The relationship between distance, speed and time can be remembered by:

$$\text{Speed (S)} = \frac{\text{Distance (D) miles}}{\text{Time (T) hour}} \quad \text{or } S = \frac{60 \times D \text{ (miles)}}{T \text{ (minutes)}}$$

Note that in the second equation, 60 converts hours to minutes

Calculating Speed. If you motored a distance of 2 nautical miles in 6 minutes, your speed would be calculated as 20 knots.

$$S = \frac{60 \times D}{T} = \frac{60 \times 2 \text{ nautical miles}}{6 \text{ minutes}} \qquad S = 20 \text{ knots}$$

Calculating Distance. If you have been motoring at 10 knots for 12 minutes, then you have run a distance of 2 miles.

$$D = \frac{S \times T}{60} = \frac{10 \text{ knots} \times 12 \text{ minutes}}{60} \qquad D = 2 \text{ miles}$$

Calculating Time. A distance of 20 miles is to be run at 15 knots. How long will the passage take?

$$T = \frac{D}{S} = \frac{20}{15} = \frac{4}{3} \qquad T = 1\frac{1}{3} \text{ hours or 1 hour and 20 minutes}$$

Direction

Almost all paper charts are oriented with North at the top ("North-up"). If you start at North and turn right round to North again, you'll swivel through 360 degrees. All direction at sea is defined in terms of these degrees by using a compass.

Which Course is Real? Unlike a car, which is traveling in one direction at a given time, a boat's movement offers three choices. All are correct, but the difference is important:

• *Heading* is the direction the boat is pointing.
• *Course Over Ground (COG or Track)* is the direction the boat is traveling in across the surface of the planet. In a crosscurrent, this may well be different from the boat's heading. Most plotters can show you either, or both. Choose, and know which you have chosen. If in doubt, go for COG.
• *Course desired* is the course you need to make good to get to where you are going.

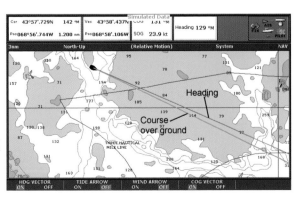

Realities of Speed. You can see your speed at a glance on most boats either by the speedometer or log (if you have one) or checking the SOG (Speed Over Ground) on the GPS. It is important to understand that the speedometer is reading the speed of the vessel *through the water*, while the GPS reads speed *across the surface* of the planet. If a current is running, GPS will include this in its SOG readout. Thus: 20 knots indicated on the speedometer when motoring into an adverse current of 2 knots leads to a SOG value of 18 knots. The same speed in a favoring current would read out as 22 knots SOG.

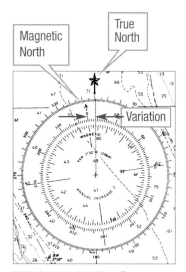

Variation can be either East or West. This example shows Magnetic North to the West of True North and is a West variation. The note inside the circles indicates a variation of 7°30" W (West).

Compass Tips

- *If a GPS gives your heading in degrees True, you will have to convert it to a magnetic heading for your compass by adding or subtracting the variation. Add for a West (W) variation and subtract for an East (E) variation.*
- *Know the position of the steering wheel for a straight course.*
- *Don't chase the compass.*
- *Motion can jostle a compass. Read it when the boat is steady.*
- *Don't stare at the compass. Have a reference to steer to, such as a buoy, a point of land, or a distant cloud.*
- *Remember the boat turns around the compass – the compass doesn't turn in the boat.*

Compass Variation. Your boat's magnetic compass points to Magnetic North, but your charts are oriented to True North. The difference in degrees between your compass readings and True North is called variation. The amount and direction of variation will change depending on your location. The compass rose on your chart will indicate the amount and direction of the variation for your area.

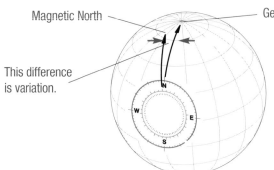

Magnetic North is not a fixed point like True North, but slowly wanders. The amount that it changes each year is also indicated on the compass rose as an annual increase or decrease.

Compass Deviation. Your compass responds to iron or steel objects which have magnetic properties. The difference in compass readings created by their magnetic influence is called the deviation. For instance, a bag of tools accidentally placed next to the compass can cause a deviation so that the compass reads 075 degrees when it should read 080 degrees. Even metal eyeglass frames can do it.

Compass Variation on a GPS. A GPS often tells you the direction to or from something. It can do this in degrees True or degrees Magnetic. It's critical to know which it is, because in some places the discrepancy can be 20 degrees or

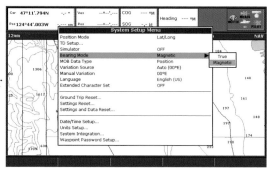

more. A menu in most GPS sets and plotters allows the user to set the instrument to readout True or Magnetic. Either is fine, but you MUST know which it is.

The Waypoint

A waypoint is a position of tactical interest chosen by the navigator. GPS will instantly give an activated waypoint's distance and bearing relative to the boat. Waypoints have many uses, some of which will be discussed in Chapter 15.

Inputting a Waypoint on a Plotter. To enter a waypoint using the plotter, open the waypoint menu, then move the cursor over the desired position on the chart for the waypoint and click on it. The plotter will automatically display the latitude and longitude numbers for the waypoint. This method avoids the potential human error problem of manually entering the lat/long numbers.

Inputting a Waypoint on a GPS from a Paper Chart. Use the chart to select the position of your desired waypoint, then determine its latitude and longitude using the method described earlier in "Plotting a Position on a Paper Chart" and input these numbers into the GPS. Once activated by pressing the GoTo button, the readout gives distance and bearing to the waypoint.

Just How Good Is GPS

At its best, GPS is far more accurate than any ordinary boater needs. However, before risking one's boat, one or two caveats must be considered.

Chart Accuracy. In many countries charts are drawn with the utmost care, generally from meticulous survey data, but there are some areas in the world where this may not be the case. While GPS at sea can deliver a position good to 49 feet or less, the lines on a chart may be thicker than that, or the survey may have been conducted before GPS with a lesser degree of assumed accuracy. An electronic chart can often be zoomed in well beyond the intentions of the surveyor. Some plotters indicate when they're over-zoomed – perhaps with dots on the chart. Many do not. The answer is always to leave a seamanlike margin for reasonable error, and give rocks a wide berth.

Satellite Coverage. Once a GPS receiver is well "warmed up," satellite coverage is rarely an issue, but the instrument is only as good as the data its antenna is receiving. Check the satellite screen before you leave your slip, and take a look every so often to make sure all is well.

Datum. In the U.S. and many other areas of the world, GPS delivers its position using a lat/long datum called WGS84 (World Geodetic System 1984). However, a GPS may produce a position which is not consistent with the paper chart in use because the chart has been drawn to an older or different datum. It is possible to check a chart's datum in the title notes, then enter the GPS menus and make sure the one selected coincides. If the GPS or the plotter doesn't seem to coincide perfectly with reality, look for the buoys, use the depth sounder, and plenty of common sense.

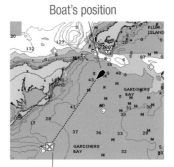

Boat's position

Waypoint

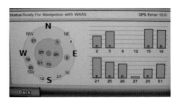

This GPS satellite screen indicates signals are being received from 9 satellites and the accuracy of the GPS position is estimated as 10.6 feet. Four satellites are needed for a 3D fix (position and altitude). The position and number of satellites will vary as the earth rotates and the satellites change their positions in orbit. Satellite signals cannot penetrate solid objects. If used below deck in a boat, an external antenna may be needed.

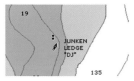

Here's a buoy on a chart plotter. For more details, place the cursor over it and press ENTER.

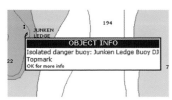

A box pops up with more information.

Aids to Navigation

Navigation aids are nautical road signs that can be used to help you determine your position, follow a safe course and to warn of dangers. Aids to navigation may be divided into two broad categories:

❶ **Buoys** are floating marks anchored (moored) in a fixed position. Buoy positions depicted on a nautical chart are approximate within the swing movement allowed by the scope of their mooring cable. Be aware they can sometimes drag from their position as a result of storms, ice or impact with a ship.

❷ **Beacons** are fixed to the sea bottom or located on shore, making them a reliable and precise aid for navigating. Beacons include daybeacons with a daymark, beacons with a light (lights), lighthouses, and ranges.

Buoys and beacons with lights can be identified by their color (red, green, white, or yellow) and rhythm (pattern of their flashes). There are a variety of rhythms displayed by various lights. Most unlit marks have reflective tape that will be picked up by your searchlight. All marks are identified on charts. Anything floating (typically a buoy) is shown at an angle from the vertical, while fixed objects are straight up and down. NOTE: This is not necessarily the case with plotter charts.

There are four different navigation marking systems used in U.S. waters:

❶ The U.S. Marking System is used on all navigable waters in the U.S., with the exception of the Mississippi River and its tributaries and the Intracoastal Waterway.

❷ The Information and Regulatory Markers used on navigable state waters and non-navigable internal state waters.

❸ The Intracoastal Waterway System used on the Intracoastal Waterway from New Jersey through Texas.

❹ The Western River System used on the Mississippi River and its tributaries.

U.S. Marking System

Lateral Marks. A system of lateral marks is used to indicate on which side a mark should be passed when returning from seaward. In U.S. waters, red marks are kept on your right (starboard) side and green ones on your left (port) side. Remember this orientation by the "3 Rs" of "RED, RIGHT, RETURNING (from seaward)." When an approach from seaward cannot be determined, the Conventional Direction is used, which is a clockwise rotation around the U.S. land mass and northerly and westerly in the Great Lakes, except for southerly in Lake Michigan.

Caution

It is illegal to tie onto an aid to navigation or be in a position that prevents other vessels from seeing it.

The Conventional Direction for lateral marks is a clockwise rotation around the U.S.

STARBOARD (RIGHT) LATERAL MARKS
Color: **RED**
Shape: **NUNS OR TRIANGLES**
Character: **EVEN NUMBERS**
Light: **RED** (if lighted)

PORT (LEFT) LATERAL MARKS
Color: **GREEN**
Shape: **CANS** or **SQUARES**
Character: **ODD NUMBERS**
Light: **GREEN** (if lighted)

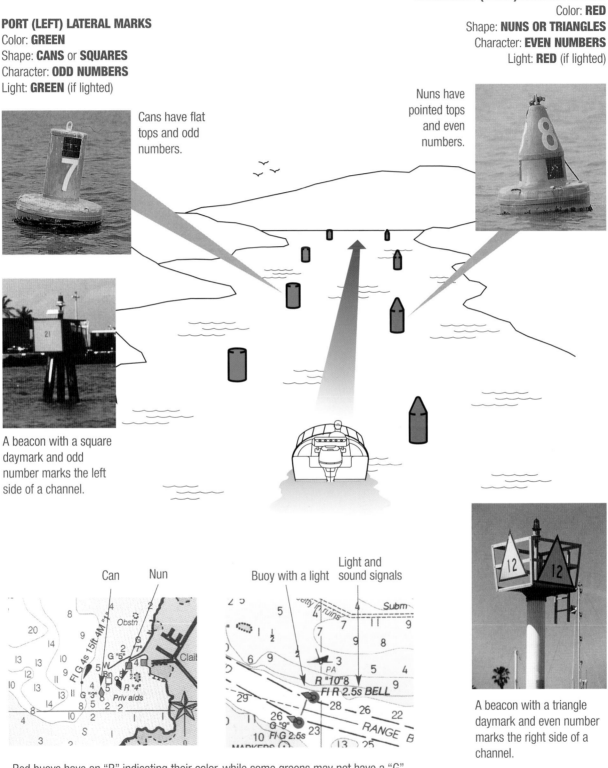

Cans have flat tops and odd numbers.

Nuns have pointed tops and even numbers.

A beacon with a square daymark and odd number marks the left side of a channel.

Can   Nun

Buoy with a light

Light and sound signals

A beacon with a triangle daymark and even number marks the right side of a channel.

Red buoys have an "R" indicating their color, while some greens may not have a "G". Note the odd number (G "3") on the green can and the even number (R "4") on the red nun. If a red or green buoy has a light and/or sound signal, this is indicated (Fl R 2.5s BELL).

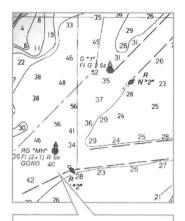

This preferred channel buoy with a light is identified on the chart by RG "MH" Fl (2+1) R 6s. The RG symbol indicates that the top band is red (R), which tells us that the preferred channel is to the left. We can also identify the buoy by the letters "MH" on it.

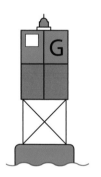

Green top band indicates the preferred channel should be passed on your port side to take the preferred channel.

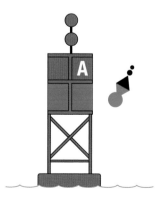

Isolated Danger Mark

Preferred Channel Marks. When channels divide, one will be "preferred" for deeper draft vessels or as part of a continuing waterway. It may or may not be the one you want, but at the division you will find a preferred channel buoy. This may be passed on either side but will exhibit a preferred side based on the color of the uppermost band. If the main channel is to your left, when returning from seaward, the top band will be red indicating the buoy is to be passed on your right (starboard) side. If the top band is green that indicates the preferred channel is to the right and the buoy is to be passed on your left (port) side.
Color: red and green horizontal bands
Shape: cans, squares, nuns, and triangles
Character: letter (s)
Light: same color as uppermost band (if lighted) and is a group flashing light, e.g., Gp Fl (2+1) 6s (2 flashes and 1 flash every 6 seconds)

Safe Water Marks. These marks denote navigable (safe) water on all sides. They are frequently used to identify the middle of a channel or an offshore approach point to a channel.
Color: red and white vertical stripes
Shape: sphere or buoy with a red spherical topmark
Character: letter (s)
Light: white (if lighted) and flashes the Morse code (Mo) signal for the letter "A" (i.e., 1 short flash followed by 1 long flash)

This lighted safe water buoy at the seaward approach to the Winyah Bay channel is identified by the symbols RW (red and white stripes) and Mo A (light flashes Morse code "A"). "WB" indicates it is the safe water mark for the Winyah Bay entrance.

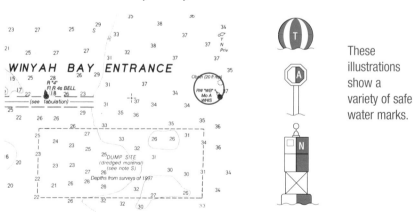

These illustrations show a variety of safe water marks.

Isolated Danger Marks. These are placed near an isolated danger with navigable water all around. They have black and red horizontal bands with a topmark of two black spheres. If lighted, they display a group flashing of two white flashes every 5 seconds.

Special Purpose Marks. These are not navigation marks, but are used to alert you to a special feature or area such as the Triton submarine turning basin at the mouth of the St. Mary's River. They also mark pipelines, traffic separation schemes, spoil areas, and jetties. These marks can be identified by their yellow color with black letter(s). If lighted, they display a yellow fixed or flashing light. You will have to refer to a chart, Notices to Mariners, Coast Pilot or Light List to determine their meaning.

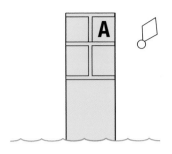

Special Purpose Mark

Lighthouses. A lighthouse is an important aid to navigation at night, but can also be used in the daytime. The chart shows them as a star with various technical data about their light and fog signals. A coast pilot book tells you what they look like. With light structures surrounded by water, note the symbol for the rip-rap which often surrounds them, and don't go too close. The same often applies to other structures such as jetties.

Information and Regulatory Markers

These are used to alert you to dangers, exclusion and controlled areas, directions, and other regulatory matters and information. They have orange square, diamond or circle symbols with an orange band above and below the symbol displayed against a white background.

Intracoastal Waterway System (ICW)

This waterway on the East Coast and the Gulf of Mexico uses its own unique markings of a yellow triangle ▲ and a yellow square ■. Since there is no obvious approach from seaward for the ICW, the Conventional Direction of clockwise rotation around the U.S. land mass is used. As a result, the marks toward the mainland side of the waterway are designated as marking the right side of the waterway by a yellow triangle ▲, and the ones toward the sea are the left side and marked with a yellow square ■. When following the ICW from New Jersey to Texas, a yellow ▲ should be left on the boat's starboard side and a yellow ■ on its port side, regardless of the color of the navigation aid on which they appear. The prudent navigator will follow charts closely and carry an up-to-date ICW cruising guide.

There are places along the Intracoastal Waterway where its waterway and a channel leading in from the sea coincide. If the directions of the two systems are the same, the yellow triangles will be on the red marks and the yellow squares on the green marks. But if the conventional direction of the ICW runs opposite to the "returning from seaward" direction of the channel, the U.S. Marking system for the channel prevails and the yellow triangles will be on the channel's

BOAT EXCLUSION AREA

Explanation may be placed outside the crossed diamond shape, such as dam, rapids, swim area, etc.

DANGER

The nature of danger may be indicated inside the diamond shape, such as rock, wreck, shoal, dam, etc.

CONTROLLED AREA

Type of control is indicated in the circle, such as slow, no wake, speed limit, etc.

green marks and the yellow squares on the red marks. Extreme care should be taken when passing the junction of the ICW and a channel leading in from the sea. The mixture of marks can be very confusing, but if you follow the yellow ICW symbols, you should not get lost.

The Intracoastal Waterway is a network of protected inland water routes winding from New Jersey to Texas.

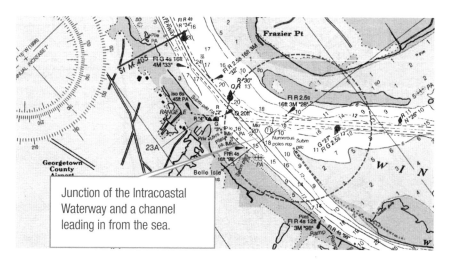

Junction of the Intracoastal Waterway and a channel leading in from the sea.

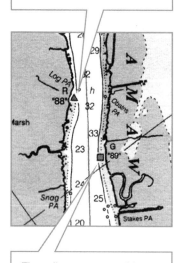

The yellow triangle on this red daymark indicates the starboard (mainland) side of the ICW channel.

The yellow square on this green daymark marks the port (seaward) side of the ICW channel.

Western River System

This is used on the Mississippi River and its tributaries above Baton Rouge as well as certain other rivers emptying into the Gulf of Mexico. Its major differences from the U.S. Marking system are:
- Aids to navigation are not numbered or lettered. Numbers on marks represent mileages.
- Safe water and isolated danger marks are not used.
- Lights on green aids show a single flashing green or white light; lights on red aids have a red or white group flashing light.
- Diamond-shaped crossing boards indicate where the channel crosses from one riverbank to the other.

REVIEW QUESTIONS

1. One minute of latitude on a Mercator chart is equal to _____nautical mile(s).
2. A boat is motoring against a current of 2 knots and its speedometer reads 15 knots, the SOG on the GPS would read _____ knots.
   a. 13 b. 15 c. 17
3. _____ is the direction a boat is pointing.
4. The difference between Magnetic North on your compass and True North on a chart is called _____.
   a. deviation b. oscillation c. variation
5. When returning from seaward, red marks are kept to the _____ side of a boat.

Answers: 1) one 2) a. 13 3) Heading 4) c. variation 5) starboard

15. Basic Navigation & Piloting

KEY CONCEPTS
▶ Plotting a position
▶ Defining track, heading & desired course
▶ Plotting a course
▶ Creating waypoints & routes
▶ Working with GPS, chart & electronic chart plotters
▶ Coping with electronic failure

When comparing GPS on the boat with GPS in the car, a parallel emerges. On the road, if GPS says you're at ramp 46 on I-95, that is where you are, but it will be a safe bet that you don't take it for granted. You look at the road signs to make absolutely sure. If there are no signs at a country junction you'll go with the GPS, but you'll feel faintly uneasy. You are executing an essential navigation concept which is, "Never believe what you're told by a single source." Check with a second, and a third if possible.

Even with modern GPS and chart plotters, mistakes remain possible – often of our own making. If you're running a GPS route, keep track of the buoys. Note each one as it goes by and take a glance at the depth sounder to make sure the depth confirms what you see. That way you're certain all is well. On land you can see danger ahead, so the double-check is a convenience, not a lifesaver. On the water, shoals or rocks may lie just under the surface. Ignore this policy, and if you've entered a dubious waypoint, the first you'll know about it will be on impact.

Determining Your Position

On a Chart Plotter or GPS. The screen shows the boat's real-time position all the time. Plotting a GPS position onto a paper chart has been described in Chapter 14. It can be checked by using a waypoint (see "Checking Accuracy" in this chapter). If your electronics go down, you'll need a backup system for determining position, and when the situation calls for precise maneuvering and leaves no room for error, it is often safer to use your eyes rather than a screen. What follows is the time-honored traditional method for plotting a position and fix without electronics.

Plotting a Bearing. An imaginary line joining a known, charted point with the boat's position is called a bearing. In the illustration, bearing **Ⓐ** has been taken of a chimney stack with a hand bearing compass. This compass reading is marked on the compass rose and transferred from the magnetic ring of the compass rose using a parallel ruler or a chart protractor. It appears as a line running from the stack. Your position is somewhere on this line (line **Ⓐ** on the chart on page 126).

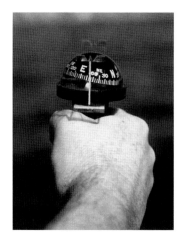

The hand bearing compass (above) is more accurate for taking bearings because you can position the object just above the numbers on the compass.

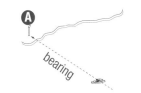

A bearing of **Ⓐ** is taken with a compass.

Additional bearings of **B** and **C** are taken to determine the boat's position.

Plotting a Fix. You can use multiple bearings (directions) to fixed objects from your boat to determine your position fairly exactly. In the example shown, bearings **A**, **B** and **C** have been taken from three objects and transferred to the chart. Since the boat is on all three lines, the boat should be at their point of intersection (called a *fix*), or was when the last bearing was taken. In practice, all three lines pass rarely through the same precise point. Instead they form a small triangle. If your fix was correctly performed with care, your position should be inside the triangle.

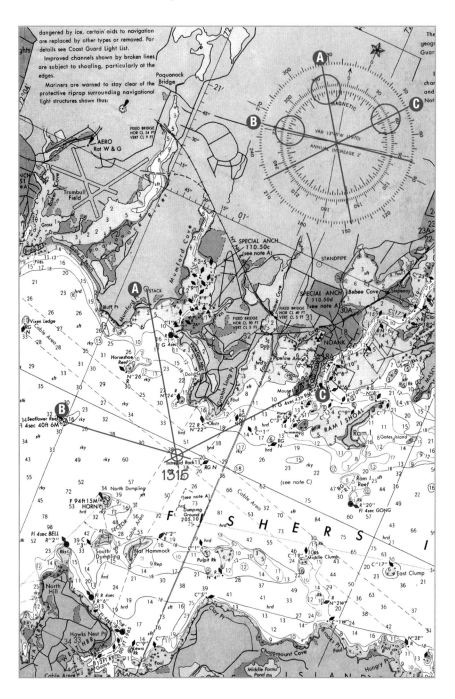

Determining a Course To Steer

On a Chart Plotter. On a plotter screen you can see where you are and where you're going. A line from one to the other can be defined in degrees as a compass heading. This gives a course to steer, so long as there are no dangers in the way. The compass heading can be found from a plotter in at least three ways:

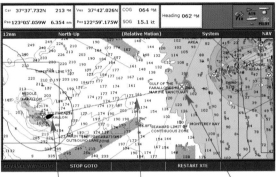

Boat's position   Course to steer line   Waypoint

Place a waypoint at your destination and activate it. On most plotters, a line will appear which will be your course to steer. You may also choose to use the split-screen option shown in the waypoint section of this chapter.

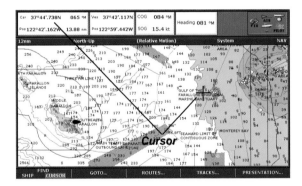

Place the cursor over the destination (black cross). The cursor data box (here at top left) will give direction (and distance) to the cursor. That's your course to the destination.

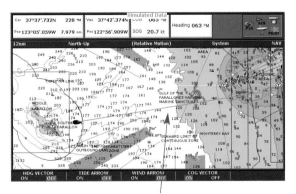

Projected track (green line)

The plotter's projected track indicates where the boat will go if you stay on this course. Steer to keep this line over the destination and you are tracking toward it. You can find the feature in the menus, and it makes good sense to have it switched on all the time. This plotter calls the line a COG Vector. It is found in the Data menus.

If there are obstacles or dangers along the track, consider planning an electronic route (see "Creating Routes" in this chapter).

Portable Plotters

Small or portable GPS units come in two essential varieties: those carrying charts and basic plotter facilities, and those which do not. The simple GPS unit works in digits only, although it may have some sort of mapping facility. In most cases, this "non-chart mapping" is of limited use. A tiny plotter, although featuring proper charts, is restricted as a navigational tool by sheer screen size, but the charting screens are handy for plotting waypoints and routes. Some of the larger portable units are big enough to pilot with, but screen size demands that they are used with a paper chart to maintain a sensible overview.

Mobile Phones and Tablets

Today's sophisticated phones and the larger tablet-sized units can operate excellent plotter programs, interfacing with their built-in GPS. The bigger the screen, the better, and unless you know an area intimately, the phone-sized ones are better used with a paper chart. Be aware that they are not waterproofed like marine GPS units and may be difficult to see in direct sunlight.

On the Paper Chart.

With a compass and chart, once you know where you are, you can determine a course to steer. For instance, you are at point **A** on the chart and want to go to point **B**. Draw a line from **A** to **B**. Make sure there are no hazards such as rocks, reefs or shallow waters along the route. Now, transfer the line **A** – **B** to the compass rose. The line has been drawn for you on the illustration. Read the circled heading at the letter B on the inner magnetic circle of the compass rose. The heading is 272 degrees Magnetic (M), which is your compass course from **A** to **B**. To steer the course you have planned, just steer to the compass heading you have plotted.

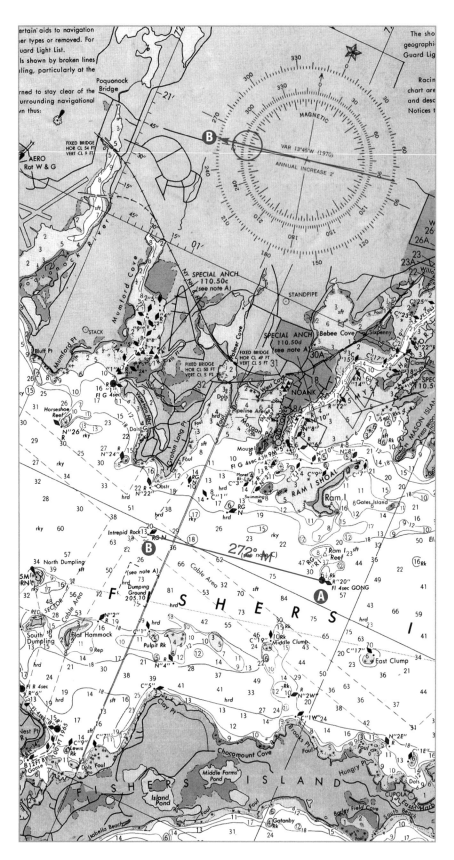

Plotting a course with parallel rulers requires "walking" the rulers across the chart to transfer information to and from the compass rose. A chart protractor does away with this inconvenience.

Creating Waypoints

Waypoints. These are how GPS handles the essential question, "How do I get to where I'm going and stay clear of trouble on the way."

Useful Waypoints.
Destination – This is a basic requirement. It supplies the data to steer to your destination and it also reads off how far it is and how long it will take to get there.

Destination waypoint

Boat's position

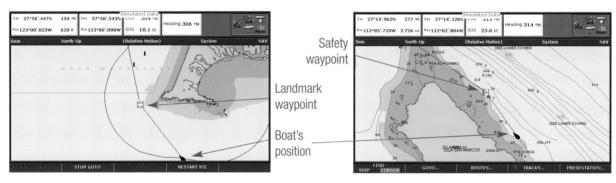

Safety waypoint

Landmark waypoint

Boat's position

Landmark – This takes you to a buoy or some other feature by which to double-check where you are.

Safety – This is placed well clear of a danger as an offset waypoint.

Working with Waypoints. The essential difference between road and water navigating (apart from the fact that the water is trackless) is that land is immovable while water slides with current. Boats also slip with wind in the form of leeway. Using waypoints properly takes care of all this.

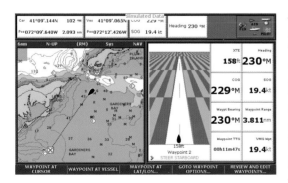

Activating a Waypoint on a Chart Plotter. This plotter has a "Waypoint" function button. The options are self-explanatory. In this case, a waypoint on a buoy has been activated by pressing "GoTo waypoint" and choosing "Waypoint 2." The split-screen format allows the data and "highway view" on the right to be followed while watching the graphic display of the chart at the same time.

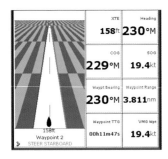

This GPS screen depicts a compass rose with a direction finding needle and indicates the COG as shown by compass heading of 322 is 27 degrees different from the bearing to the waypoint (orange arrow). The Cross-Track Error shows the boat is 109 feet to the right of the track. To steer directly to the waypoint the two needles should coincide. Note that COG as shown on most GPSs is a track history and may lag behind your current heading.

Activating a Waypoint on a Hand-Held GPS. This screen is basically the same as the one on the plotter except that there is no chart. Note the following:

- The "highway view" on the left shows at a glance if you are off-track.
- The COG (Course Over Ground) of 229 degrees is 1 degrees different from the waypoint bearing of 230 degrees. To hit the waypoint dead center, COG and bearing should be the same. Steer to make them so.
- The highway view tells you which way to alter (at the bottom of the screen). Don't forget that your heading and the COG may not be the same thing. Any crosscurrent will affect COG but not heading.
- The Waypoint Range (distance) and Waypoint TTG (time to go) boxes speak for themselves.
- SOG (Speed Over Ground) is the speed you have made over a track, while VMG (Velocity Made Good) is the speed you have made toward your destination. If you are proceeding along your desired course they will be almost the same. If they are not, this is explained by a current.
- XTE (Cross-Track Error) tells you the distance and direction you have drifted off-track since you activated the waypoint. Some units allow you to re-set this to zero – after you've checked that the new course to the waypoint doesn't take you near any dangers. This can be one of the most valuable sources of information provided by the GPS. It is possible to have drifted off track yet still be heading directly for your waypoint, but now with an obstruction or shoal ahead.

One of the greatest pitfalls in GPS navigation is simply to follow a waypoint whose bearing is changing. The track may have been fine to start with, but the new one generated by your drift might be leading you onto the rocks. Mind your cross-track error.

Checking Accuracy. By far the greatest source of GPS-related accidents is wrong data entered into it. Here's the best way to ensure your waypoints are correct. Make the lat/long entry at your home berth – you know exactly where this is on the chart. Next, hit the "GoTo" button and read off the bearing and distance to the waypoint from your known position on the screen. Now lay these off on the paper chart. If the position is on top of the plotted waypoint, you're in good shape. Otherwise, take another look at those numbers. Once a waypoint has been proven like this, you can use it in the same way to check a plotted lat/long fix out on the water.

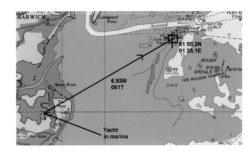

Creating Routes

The navigator on a rapidly moving powerboat doesn't always have time to plot waypoints while underway. It's better to do it beforehand. A route on either GPS or a chart plotter strings together a series of pre-planned waypoints which define the trip. Once activated, when the boat reaches Waypoint 2, the instrument clicks over to Waypoint 3 automatically, and so on. On a plotter you can watch the boat moving from one to the next and steer to keep her on the line. The GPS switches waypoints as they come up and gives you the course to steer for the next. Depending on how the screens are set up, it may also deliver course corrections to keep the boat dead on track.

Creating a Route on a Plotter. Is a matter of going into the route menu and following on-screen instructions. Each waypoint is readily clicked in with the cursor. This short sample route was set up in a couple of minutes and saved as Route 1. What we see here is the plotter zoomed out for an overview. When actually placing the waypoints, it was zoomed in for safety.

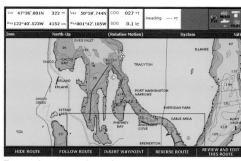
Zoomed out overview of route

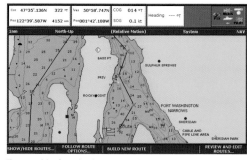
Zoomed in for placing waypoints

Setting a Route on a GPS with a Paper Chart. Each route waypoint must be plotted manually and its coordinates transferred to the GPS. With any but the simplest of routes, the process is laborious and full of potential human error. They are generally set up for regular passages, and only then are they really worth the trouble.

When the Screens Go Blank

So long as you've been keeping an eye on your position, losing the electronics doesn't mean you need assistance. Here's what to do:

When Navigating with a GPS and a Paper Chart. Always be sure to make notes in pencil as you pass important objects. What the time was is critical, and if you have a distance-reading log, note the distance too. If the GPS goes down five minutes after you passed a known buoy doing 12 knots, you've traveled a mile along the course you're steering. Plot a 1-mile line in that direction on the chart, and you're at the end of it. It is called a Dead Reckoning (DR) position. Make a note of the DR on the chart, plot a new course while looking out for landmarks.

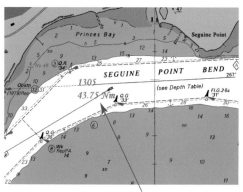
Time and distance noted at buoy.

When Navigating with a Plotter. Even when the primary navigation tool is a good plotter, it remains vital to have paper charts on board – in case it fails, as well as to maintain a better overview. In addition, navigators relying on plotters should keep a paper ship's log book to record hourly positions and other useful data. Any format will do, so long as you can understand it. Then, if the plotter dies and backup fails, you will know where you were an hour ago at worst. From that position, carry on as per the "GPS and a Paper Chart" navigator in the previous paragraph.

Mobile phones with built-in GPS and chart apps also serve as an excellent backup, assuming you're within coverage range. Make sure you have extra batteries in case you can't recharge the phone.

Running a Range

In medium and large-scale piloting, GPS or a plotter will give you what you need to keep dead on track. In tighter situations where a navigator needs to be looking around rather than staring into a screen, or in a strong crosscurrent, there is absolutely nothing to beat a range. A range is formed by lining up two fixed objects on the same bearing. The objects may be headlands, trees, buildings, towers, beacons, buoys or special range markers. You can use a range to follow a channel, keep in safe water or stay on course.

If you are motoring across a current toward a destination, you need to adjust your course to compensate for the current's effect. You can determine how much to compensate by using a range.

REVIEW QUESTIONS

1. The direction from a boat's position to a charted point or waypoint is called a _____.
2. _____ tells you the distance and direction you have drifted off-track since the waypoint was activated.
3. COG reads 220 degrees and the waypoint bearing is 230 degrees, it indicates the boat is _____ degrees off course and has to be turned to _____ to bring it back on course.
4. A series of pre-planned waypoints for a trip is called a _____.
5. Lining up two fixed objects on the same bearing is called a _____.

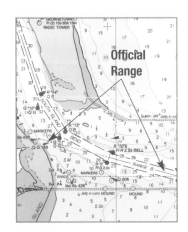

By lining up the two markers of this "official" range, you will be able to stay in the middle of the channel.

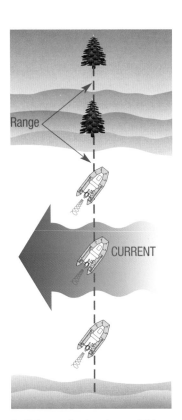

By lining up the two trees of this "natural" range, you will be able to reach your destination in a straight line.

Answers: 1) bearing 2) Cross-track error 3) 10; starboard 4) route 5) range

16. Health, Safety & Emergencies

KEY CONCEPTS
- ▶ Cold water immersion & hypothermia
- ▶ Heat emergencies
- ▶ Hazards
- ▶ PIW rescues
- ▶ Disabled boat emergencies

It is good seamanship to be prepared and able to deal with any emergency, should it occur.

Cold Water Immersion & Hypothermia

While the effects of cold water immersion and hypothermia can take place in a water temperature below 77 degrees Fahrenheit, they are most noticeable when the temperature falls below 59 degrees. Studies indicate that people are more likely to die from the initial reaction to cold water immersion than from hypothermia. The wearing of life jackets and carrying communication devices can help increase the odds of survival and rescue.

Phrase 1 – Cold Shock Response (lasts about 1 minute) – Falling into cold water produces reflex gasping, hyperventilation, and a rapid increase in heart rate and blood pressure, which could lead to a heart attack in some people. If you're not wearing a life jacket and your head goes below the water, you could inhale water and drown. Action: keep your head out of the water; get your breathing under control; don't panic.

Phase 2 – Cold Incapacitation (occurs during next 10 minutes in very cold water) – Loss of muscle coordination and strength in fingers, arms and legs occurs. Wearing a life jacket will keep you afloat and help reduce heat loss. Action: get out of the water as soon as possible since body heat loss is much greater in the water than in the air; call for help.

Phrase 3 – Hypothermia (full effect with loss of consciousness occurs in about 1 hour in very cold water) – Hypothermia occurs when the temperature of the body core drops below normal. It can also occur during prolonged exposure to cool air and/or cool spray or precipitation. Signals include shivering in the early stages, lack of shivering in the later stages, impaired judgment, dizziness, numbness, and loss of consciousness. Action: if in water, minimize loss of heat by assuming the H.E.L.P position or Huddle group position; if on a boat, replace wet clothing with dry clothing and blanket and warm gradually.

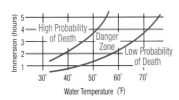

The danger of hypothermia increases as water temperature declines and the duration of immersion increases.

Chart Courtesy of U.S. Coast Guard

1 – 10 – 1 Principle of Cold Water Survival

1 minute – to get your breathing under control.
10 minutes – of meaningful movement for self-rescue.
1 hour – before you become unconscious due to hypothermia (less time if not wearing a life jacket).

H.E.L.P. position minimizes heat loss when submerged in water.

Post-Rescue. After a person is rescued, blood pressure can drop suddenly, causing heart problems; and the lungs may be damaged from water. Get medical assistance as soon as possible. Until medical arrives, follow the treatment steps listed in the hypothermia table below.

Hypothermia Prevention. Wear a life jacket and layered clothing suitable for the conditions. Best prevention in cold water includes wearing a dry suit or wet suit. Capsizing and falling overboard are the causes for most in-water hypothermia situations. To reduce these risks: don't overload a boat or shift weight too much to a side; don't go out in conditions unsuitable for your boat; avoid use of alcohol; and don't reach too far over the side of a boat.

HYPOTHERMIA

SIGNALS...
▶ Shivering
▶ Impaired judgment
▶ Dizziness
▶ Numbness
▶ Change in level of consciousness
▶ Weakness
▶ Glassy stare
(Physical symptoms may vary, since age, body size, and clothing will cause individual differences.)

TREATMENT...
Medical assistance should be given to anyone with hypothermia. Until medical assistance arrives, these steps should be taken:
▶ Check breathing and pulse.
▶ Gently move the person to a warm place.
▶ Carefully remove all wet clothing. Gradually warm person by wrapping in blankets or putting on dry clothes. Do not warm person too quickly, such as immersing in warm water. Rapid rewarming may cause dangerous heart rhythms. Hot water bottles and chemical heat packs may be used if wrapped in a towel or blanket before applying.
▶ Give warm, nonalcoholic and decaffeinated liquids to a conscious person only.

Heat Emergencies

Heat emergencies can also be life threatening. High temperature and humidity are the usual culprits. Be alert for signals whenever the temperature is around 90 degrees Fahrenheit and the relative humidity is more than 70%. Young children and elderly people are particularly vulnerable. The best preventive measure is to avoid dehydration by drinking plenty of water at regular intervals and staying in the shade.

HEAT EXHAUSTION

SIGNALS...
▶ Cool, moist, pale skin
▶ Heavy sweating
▶ Headache
▶ Dizziness
▶ Nausea
▶ Weakness, exhaustion

TREATMENT...
Without prompt care, heat exhaustion can advance to a more serious condition — heat stroke. First aid includes:
▶ Move person to cool environment.
▶ Remove clothing soaked with perspiration and loosen any tight clothing.
▶ Apply cool, wet towels or sheets.
▶ Fan the person.
▶ Give person a half glass (4 oz.) of cool water every 15 min.

Hazards

Electrical Hazards. When using electrical power tools near water or stringing extension cords along docks, make sure they are properly grounded and the power cords and connections do not make contact with the water. Overhead power lines can be a dangerous hazard. If they are touched by a long antenna, fishing rod, or some other tall metal object on your boat, the result could be shock or even electrocution. Look upward for power lines in boat launching sites or over water where they could be low-lying. Another potential electrical hazard is snagging your anchor on underwater electrical cables. Check for cable markings on shore or cable location symbols on your chart before anchoring.

Carbon Monoxide Hazards. Carbon monoxide gas is very difficult to detect because it is odorless, tasteless, and colorless. If you smell exhaust fumes from an engine, carbon monoxide (CO) is present. Exposure to CO gas can kill you at low concentrations over prolonged duration or high concentrations in a very short time. The best detection for this poisonous gas is a regularly inspected marine-approved carbon monoxide detector in spaces where CO may collect. Symptoms of carbon monoxide poisoning include headache, nausea, dizziness, weakness and irritated eyes, and are often confused with seasickness or alcohol intoxication.

Carbon monoxide gas is generated from the combustion or burning of carbon-based fuels which include gasoline, oil, propane and charcoal. Sources include: exhaust leaks or outlets from engines and generators, space heaters, water heaters, grills and propane stoves. Prevention includes: don't swim or sit near exhaust outlets while engines or generators are operating; avoid sitting in areas where wind can carry the gas; don't ride close behind a moving boat either by hanging onto the swim platform or on a short tow; avoid exhaust emissions when docked or rafted alongside another boat; ensure adequate fresh air circulation all through the boat; perform regular inspection and maintenance of engines and generators and their exhaust systems.

Propeller Strikes. Recent statistics indicate that 4% of fatalities are caused by strikes from propellers, but a propeller can also produce serious injuries. Bowriding and sitting on the gunwale of a moving boat increases the risk of falling overboard and getting hit by the propeller. To prevent runaway situations, the safety lanyard to the ignition cutoff switch (or remote wireless device) should be attached to the operator. When approaching a person in the water, the operator should keep the person in sight at all times, and when close, shut off the engine.

Action Plan for Electrical Injury
- *Never approach a victim of an electrical injury until you are sure the power is turned off.*
- *If a power line is down, wait for the fire department and/or power company.*
- *Contact a doctor or EMS personnel immediately.*
- *The victim may have breathing difficulties or be in cardiac arrest. Provide care for any life threatening conditions.*

Backflow from a low-head dam can hold a boat against the face of the dam and capsize it.

Dams. Can present a very confusing and often misleading appearance to the boater. Many larger dams incorporate hydroelectric generating plants, road crossings, and in some cases, bypass locks that allow boats to travel around the dam. These large dams are usually well marked and quite obvious. Other dams are not so obvious. Dams that allow the water to flow out of the bottom can trap an unsuspecting boat against the wall by the strong downward flow of the water. Low-head dams are designed to maintain a minimum water level upstream. To the unsuspecting boater upstream of the dam, it cannot be seen by the water flowing over it. Any boater who is downstream of the dam could get caught in the back-flow circulation and be pinned against the dam with the risk of a possible capsizing. Know the locations of these dams to avoid them.

Capsizing & Swamping. Most capsizes occur from improper loading with too much weight or improper weight distribution. Ensure that the maximum loading on the boat's maximum capacities label is not exceeded and that the boat is loaded evenly fore and aft and from side to side. It is equally important not to overpower a boat with too large an engine. With a powerful outboard or stern drive, a boat can roll significantly if turned too sharply with a sudden burst of power at slow speed. On smaller boats, this could be enough to swamp or capsize them.

Should a capsize occur the cardinal rule is to, "Stay with the boat; don't swim for shore." An overturned boat is much more easily sighted than a swimmer. Everyone should be wearing a life jacket. Be aware that a person in the water under duress weakens very quickly. After a capsize, a head count and safety check should be taken to make sure everyone is alright and wearing a life jacket. If life jackets are not available, use improvised floating aids such as paddles, floorboards, ice coolers or buoyant containers.

Overboard Prevention. Next to capsizing, falling overboard is the second leading cause of fatal boating accidents. It is also one of the most preventable. Many overboard situations occur before the boat even leaves the dock. Typically, these situations occur when passengers attempt to step aboard while carrying items and slip, or they step on the edge of the boat and lose their balance when the boat tips. Overboard incidents can also happen when people stand up or ride on the boat's bow, gunwales (outer edges) or seatbacks, or are thrown off balance by a careless driver making erratic or sudden changes in speed or direction. To help prevent falling overboard, use footwear with good traction and follow the maxim, "One hand for the boat and one hand for yourself."

Person-In-Water Rescues

Rescue Procedure. Rescuing a person in the water (PIW) is a four-stage procedure: make physical contact with PIW; attach PIW to boat; get PIW back aboard; and aftercare.

Make Physical Contact with PIW.

❶ If a person falls overboard, immediately swing stern and propeller away from PIW. Shout "Crew Overboard!" and throw buoyant objects such as cushions and life rings toward the PIW as soon as possible. Even if these objects do not come to the aid of the PIW, they will "litter the water" where he or she went overboard and help your spotter to keep the PIW in sight.

❷ Designate someone to spot and point to the PIW in the water. The spotter should NEVER take his or her eyes off the PIW.

❸ Maneuver the boat to a position downwind of the PIW, staying close enough to the PIW to keep him or her in sight while allowing sufficient room to complete the maneuver.

❹ Approach slowly using intermittent power, bow first, pointing into wind and waves with the PIW on the driver's side. This allows better visibility for the driver. Communicate with and reassure the PIW.

❺ Shift into neutral and coast to PIW, making physical contact with a paddle, boat hook or line. Turn off the engine once reliable contact has been made or if there is any risk of the PIW coming close to the propeller. Keep reassuring the PIW.

Race Track Rescue Procedure

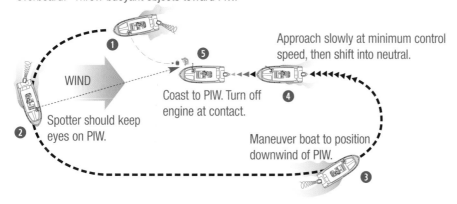

Swing stern away from victim and shout "crew overboard!" Throw buoyant objects toward PIW.

Approach slowly at minimum control speed, then shift into neutral.

WIND

Spotter should keep eyes on PIW.

Coast to PIW. Turn off engine at contact.

Maneuver boat to position downwind of PIW.

Attach PIW to Boat. Pass a Lifesling (if available) or a looped line around the PIW and attach it to the boat. This will ensure that you don't lose the PIW if he or she weakens and cannot hold on any longer. If the PIW is wearing a safety harness, attach the safety line to the harness and secure to the boat.

Get PIW Back Aboard. This can be the most difficult part of the process. Many boats may have a swimming platform and ladder on the transom. If your boat doesn't, carry a portable ladder. Some people use the stern drive or cavitation plate as a step, but there is a risk of slipping and getting cut by the propeller. Also if the PIW needs help the engine may be an obstacle. On large powerboats with high sides, a strap or sling can be rigged to lift a PIW horizontally. If there are any problems getting the PIW aboard or there is a grave and imminent threat to his or her life, activate the DSC Distress button, or make a "MAYDAY" distress call to the Coast Guard on your VHF radio, or call 911 on your cellular phone (if within response area of 911).

Aftercare. Take the greatest care of rescued a PIW who often will be suffering from varying degrees of hypothermia. Refer to the beginning of this chapter for suggested treatment.

The Lifesling is a floating collar attached to the boat by a length of floating line that doubles as a hoisting sling to retrieve a PIW in the water.

Lifesling Rescue Procedure

❶ If a person falls overboard, immediately swing stern and propeller away from PIW. Shout "Crew Overboard!" and throw buoyant objects such as cushions and life rings toward the PIW as soon as possible. Assign a spotter to watch and point at PIW.

❷ Deploy the Lifesling by opening the bag and dropping the sling into the water. It will trail out behind and draw out the remaining line.

❸ Circle the boat around the PIW with the line and sling trailing astern (similar to circling a towline to a waterskier in the water). Take care not to run over the floating line.

❹ Contact is made with the PIW by the line and sling being drawn inward by the boat's circling motion. The PIW then places the sling over head and under arms, and fastens the snap.

❺ Upon contact, shift into neutral. Once the PIW is in the Lifesling, *shut off* the engine and pull the PIW close to the boat.

❻ Set up boarding equipment and bring PIW aboard the boat and administer aftercare.

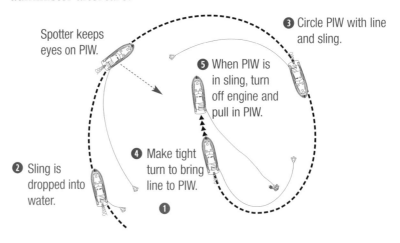

Williamson Turn Rescue Procedure

If a person falls overboard and the situation makes it difficult to keep the person in sight, the Williamson Turn is the best method to use to return back along your track to the position where he disappeared. During the maneuver, maintain constant speed throughout the turns to keep the radius of turn constant. Try to use other references than the compass to avoid acceleration errors in the compass during the turns.

Disabled Boat

Running Aground. The severity of this situation depends on how fast the boat was moving and the hardness of the ground. The combination of high speed and a hard, rocky bottom can cause extensive damage to the hull, as well as serious injury to occupants. Slow and soft impact is most likely an uneventful self-rescue situation. After running aground, make a full damage assessment and check for leaks before freeing the boat. If the boat is holed you may not want to float free until you've stopped the flow of water.

Generally, when boats with outboards or stern drives hit bottom, the skeg and propeller will be the first to strike. If the neoprene hub (or shear pin) is still intact, you may be able to free the boat by quickly reducing the throttle to idle rpm and then shifting into neutral. Next tilt the outboard motor into the shallow water position and try to carefully back off in the direction you came from. Strong backing thrust from the propeller may pile sand up, blocking the hull from moving backward. Another alternative is to move everyone forward to raise the stern and push the boat off with a paddle. If the neoprene hub is damaged, you'll be able to run the outboard, but only at low power.

❸ Turn in the opposite direction through 270 degrees.

❹ When turn is completed, proceed back along original course.

❷ Turn left (or right) through 90 degrees.

❶ Person falls overboard.

❶ Reduce throttle to idle rpm and shift into neutral.

❷ Tilt outboard to shallow water position and shift into reverse to back off.

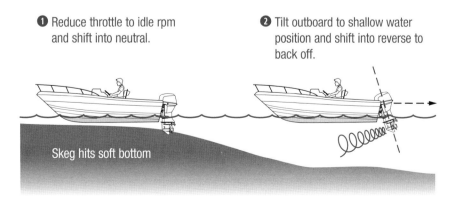

Skeg hits soft bottom

Action Plan for Running Aground
- *Check crew for possible injury.*
- *Determine damage to boat.*
- *Attempt to free boat without causing further damage.*

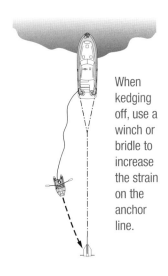

When kedging off, use a winch or bridle to increase the strain on the anchor line.

If the boat is firmly stuck and the tide is rising, the best course may be to get an anchor out in the direction of deep water and keep a strain on it, and wait while the tide floats the boat off.

An anchor can also be used to help pull your boat free *(kedge off)*. It can be placed in position by carrying it out in a small inflatable boat, or floating it with cushions or extra life jackets and swimming it out. Keep a strain on it the whole time you are attempting to free the boat. When the boat breaks free, take up on the line and keep it clear of the propeller.

If you cannot get off, you'll need the assistance of a professional towboat rescue service. If another boater offers to help, use great caution. Lines used to pull a grounded boat clear are put under tremendous strain as well as the chocks and cleats. Cleats on small pleasure boats frequently cannot withstand such loads. If a line should break or a cleat pulls away, injury can result.

Action Plan for Flooding
If flooding occurs, make sure everyone is wearing a life jacket and follow these three steps:
1. *Start pumping and bailing with large solid bucket.*
2. *Locate leak.*
3. *Stop the flow. You may be able to raise the damaged area above the waterline by shifting equipment and people. Pack a hole with some sort of plugging material, such as a shirt, extra life jackets, cushions or even a nerf ball. This temporary remedy may slow the water flow enough to slowly head for a near shore where the boat can be beached.*

If you cannot stem the flooding, this is the time to use your distress signals and push the DSC Distress button, or call the Coast Guard on Channel 16 of your VHF radio.

Flooding. If a boat is taking on water, it could be caused by damage to the hull from hitting an underwater object or crashing off waves at high speeds. Many outboard-driven powerboats have double hulls. If the operator suspects an impact was hard enough to damage the outer hull, every effort should be made to determine whether the space between the hulls is flooding. Another possibility is failure of a through-hull fitting, such as a seacock. An inboard engine offers additional possibilities, such as a broken hose line in its cooling system, a torn outdrive boot or a leaking seal at the stern tube on a "fixed" propeller drive system.

Engine Failure. When a boat suddenly loses power and starts drifting, consider whether or not it is in danger. Quickly determine if it is drifting toward rocks, shallow waters or a heavy-traffic shipping channel.
- If there is no danger and you're drifting in safe waters, the best alternative may be to try to fix the problem or call the local towboat rescue service.
- If the water is shallow enough for anchoring, this could be the best alternative until help arrives. Being anchored in a fixed place will also make it easier for the towing service to find you.
- If land is nearby or the wind is favorable, another alternative may be to paddle the boat or even rig a sail from the boat's canopy. Remember, it is always safer to stay with the boat and not attempt to swim for help.

If you cannot fix the problem, you can call the local towing service on the VHF radio channel it monitors or via a cellular phone. You can also use the appropriate distress signals on board your boat to attract the attention of another boat (see Chapter 10). You should not activate the DSC Distress button or make a "MAYDAY" distress call to the U.S. Coast Guard unless there is a grave and imminent (actually happening) danger to the vessel or the life of a person(s) on board.

Fire. Nothing can be more frightening than the sudden outbreak of a fire on board. The importance of strategically placed and fully charged fire extinguishers cannot be overly stressed (see Chapter 10 for fire extinguishers requirements). The most effective way of preventing a fire is ensuring that fuel and gear are stowed properly and that bilges are kept clean.

Most fires can be controlled providing the boater acts immediately and properly. Know how to use your fire extinguisher and take the opportunity to practice its use. When using an extinguisher, sweep its discharge across the base of the flames and keep going until the extinguisher is empty. Watch the remnants for re-ignition. An easy way to remember proper procedure in an emergency situation is the acronym PASS: **P**ull pin, **A**im at fire base, **S**queeze handle, **S**weep side to side using short bursts.

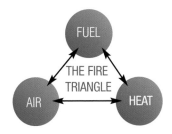

Some form of fuel, heat and air are the three elements necessary for fire to occur.

Types of Fires	Extinguishing Methods
Class A: wood, paper, cloth, rubber, some plastics	1. Water, poured or hosed, on flames 2. Dry chemical extinguisher 3. Fire blanket for contained galley fires 4. FE-241, FM-200 automatic extinguishers (Halon replacements)
Class B: flammable liquids including diesel, oil, gasoline, alcohol	1. Dry chemical extinguisher 2. Carbon dioxide (CO_2) extinguisher 3. FE-241, FM-200 automatic extinguishers
Class C: live electrical fires	1. Carbon dioxide (CO_2) extinguisher 2. Dry chemical extinguisher 3. FE-241, FM-200 automatic extinguishers

Towing and Being Towed

There are professional towboat rescue services in many areas that will respond to your request for a tow. They can be reached by VHF radio or cellular phone. Keep their telephone numbers on board your boat in case you need to call them. If you ever need a tow or have to help another boat in trouble, consider the following:

Action Plan for Fire
- The first person to see a fire should shout "Fire!" and everyone should move on deck wearing a life jacket.
- Steer the boat so as to lessen any wind and to keep the smoke clear of people on board.
- If danger seems imminent and life-threatening, use your distress signals and activate the DSC Distress button, or make a "MAYDAY" distress call to the Coast Guard on Channel16 of your VHF radio, or a 911 call on your cellular phone (if within response area of 911).
- Prepare to abandon the boat.

Towing Tips

- *Operator of towboat briefs boat to be towed and a means of communication (i.e., hand signals or VHF radio) is established.*
- *Start the tow slowly, maintaining a steady strain on the towline, and tow at a moderate, safe speed.*
- *Adjust the length of the towline so that both boats climb up and slide down waves at the same time.*
- *Make wide turns.*
- *Avoid bow-down trim to maintain steering control.*
- *On the boat being towed, raise the outboard motor to the "up" position and lock it. If the boat weaves out of control, you may have to lower motor to help it track, which will require a much slower towing speed.*
- *Steer towed boat with rudder to follow behind towboat.*
- *Allow plenty of time for the tow to slow down before attempting to release the tow.*
- *Be prepared to shorten up on the towline when entering an anchorage.*
- *Tow to the nearest safe anchorage, harbor or marina.*

- A towline of 100 feet of 1/2-inch or 5/8-inch double braided nylon is recommended. If an anchor line is used, make sure it is in good condition. If nylon line breaks under load, it has a dangerous whipping action.
- If there is no towing eye, rig a bridle (see detail) to split the load. If the reliability of the cleats or eyes are questionable, it may be necessary to wrap the towline completely around the boat.
- Do not stand near or in line with the towline and bridle, in case it breaks or cleats pull out.
- Everyone should wear a life jacket.

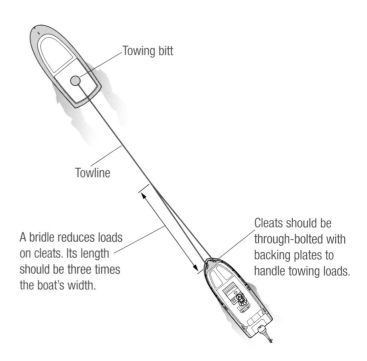

Towing bitt

Towline

A bridle reduces loads on cleats. Its length should be three times the boat's width.

Cleats should be through-bolted with backing plates to handle towing loads.

REVIEW QUESTIONS

1. *If your boat capsizes, you should _____ the boat.*
   a. leave b. recover c. anchor d. stay with
2. *To recover a person from the water it is best to approach from _____ of the person.*
3. *If your boat experiences engine failure and you are not in grave and imminent danger you should _____.*
   a. swim to shore b. tie onto a channel buoy c. stay with the boat
   d. make a Mayday call
4. *When using a fire extinguisher, sweep the discharge across the _____ of the flames.*
5. *To extinguish a diesel or gasoline fire, you should use _____.*
   a. water b. a fire blanket c. a wet chemical extinguisher
   d. a dry chemical extinguisher

Answers: 1) d. stay with 2) downwind 3) c. stay with the boat 4) base 5) d. a dry chemical extinguisher

17. Launching & Trailering

KEY CONCEPTS

▶ Trailering   ▶ Hoist operation
▶ Ramp launching & hauling out

A boat on a trailer expands the range of boating opportunities, and your ability to easily use a ramp or hoist will add to the enjoyment of your on-water experience. Preparation and a little maneuvering practice with your vehicle and trailer are the keys to success.

Trailering

The combined weight of boat and trailer affects the vehicle in several ways:

❶ its ability to pull and stop;

❷ weight on the hitch may depress the vehicle's rear suspension where the front wheels become light on the road, making it difficult to steer and blinding oncoming drivers with high headlights;

❸ additional wear on brakes, transmission, suspension and tires as well as possible engine overheating.

Check the owner's manual (or contact a dealer) for manufacturer's limits, towing weight limitations, warranty requirements and suggested packages for towing.

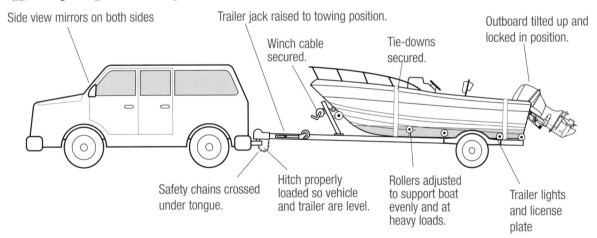

Side view mirrors on both sides

Trailer jack raised to towing position.

Winch cable secured.

Tie-downs secured.

Outboard tilted up and locked in position.

Safety chains crossed under tongue.

Hitch properly loaded so vehicle and trailer are level.

Rollers adjusted to support boat evenly and at heavy loads.

Trailer lights and license plate

Trailer Inspection

Trailer Hitches. Conventional hitches come in five classifications (I, II, III, IV, V) that are rated for different gross trailer weights and tongue weights. Avoid hitches attached to bumpers. The weight on a hitch ball (tongue weight) typically ranges from 5% to 10% of the combined weight of the trailer and boat with fuel and gear. If the

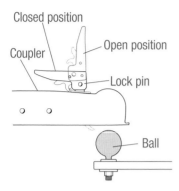

Closed position

Coupler

Open position

Lock pin

Ball

Ball should match coupler size and should be lightly greased. There are three ball sizes: 1 7/8 inches (typically rated for 2,000 pounds), 2 inches (rated anywhere from 3,500 pounds to 6,000 pounds), and 2 5/16 inches (6,000 to 10,000 pounds). The coupler usually has the ball size marked on it along with the maximum gross weight and maximum tongue weight (combined weight of the trailer and boat on the ball).

Spare Parts List

- Spare trailer bearings, seals and grease
- Spare trailer tire
- Spare bulbs for trailer lights
- Trailer jack and lug wrench
- Spare tie-downs and lines

tongue weight is too light, the trailer can swerve back and forth ("fishtail") on the road. If it's too heavy, the vehicle will be difficult to steer.

Safety Chains. Safety chains should be used and crossed under the tongue and attached to the vehicle's frame. They should not drag on the ground or come under tension when making a tight turn.

Tires & Brakes. Tires (including spare) should be inflated to recommended pressure and trailer brakes checked to insure they are working properly. Brakes are activated either electrically or with a surge hydraulic system. Each type has its pros and cons. Check your state law and talk with experienced boaters in your area to determine what type best meets your needs. Many states require trailer brakes when the combined weight of the trailer and boat exceeds 3,000 lbs, but the limit can go as low as 1,500 lbs.

Wheel Bearings. Check wheel bearings for signs of wear (each side of the hub has a bearing). Signs of worn bearings are: noise as wheel rotates, wheel wobble, smoke or excessive heat at the hub, or grease residue sprayed on wheel or boat. Bearings should be removed and checked every 1,000 miles or at the beginning of each season. Waterproof bearings and/or spring-loaded bearing protector caps are recommended. Lubricate the bearings with marine-grade waterproof grease, being careful not to use too much.

Boat Support. Be sure roller supports or bunks (pads) support boat evenly along centerline, near chine and at transom, and at locations where weight is concentrated. Secure gear to prevent movement and lock outboard or stern drive in towing position. Make sure tie-downs are snug and secured. Drain plugs should be removed and stowed.

Driving Tips While Trailering

- *Allow extra time and space to accelerate and stop.*
- *When slowing down or stopping, gradually increase pressure on trailer and car brakes. Avoid hitting the brakes hard. This is especially dangerous on wet roads and could jackknife the trailer. Sudden stops while turning may also jackknife the trailer.*
- *If the trailer starts to fishtail, minimize steering and slowly reduce speed until the fishtailing stops.*
- *When driving downhill, shift into lower gear to avoid excessive brake wear.*
- *When turning, make a wider turning radius to prevent the trailer from hitting an obstacle on the inside of your turn. Use the rear-view mirror to check trailer clearance to the obstacle.*
- *In windy or truck-passing conditions, trailers may have a tendency to fishtail. Tow at a slower speed in these conditions.*

- *Reduce speed for bumps or depressions in the road.*
- *When backing a trailer, avoid over-steering. Turn the bottom of the steering wheel in the direction you want the back of the trailer to turn.*
- *Some states have lower speed limits for trailering.*
- *Check the trailer, boat and tie-downs periodically.*

Launching

❶ Get the boat ready to launch in an area that does not block the ramp. Insert and secure drain plugs, remove tie-downs (except for winch cable), unplug wiring connector, add boat gear, attach bow and stern lines, connect fuel line attachments, and complete starting checks. Allow the trailer's wheel bearings and lights to cool before launching to avoid damaging them by sudden cooling.

❷ Back trailer slowly down ramp until boat is in water. Use rear-view mirrors to keep both sides of ramp in view when backing. Know where the end of the ramp stops to avoid running the trailer's wheels off it. Many ramps have a mark to indicate its end. Avoid immersing the vehicle's exhaust pipes in the water. A tongue extension may be required to launch deeper draft boats or for shallow slope ramps.

❸ Park in first or "park" gear and place a chock behind the vehicle's rear wheel.

❹ Have someone take the bow line so the boat won't float away.

❺ Detach the winch cable from the boat.

❻ Start the boat and back away.

❼ Remove the vehicle and trailer from the ramp as soon as possible.

CAUTION: Be aware of slippery ramps. They can cause injury or make it difficult for vehicles with or without four-wheel drive to pull a boat up the ramp. Before launching, open a window in case the vehicle accidentally slips off the ramp and becomes submerged.

Turn Right

When backing a trailer, turn the bottom of the steering wheel in the direction you want the trailer to turn.

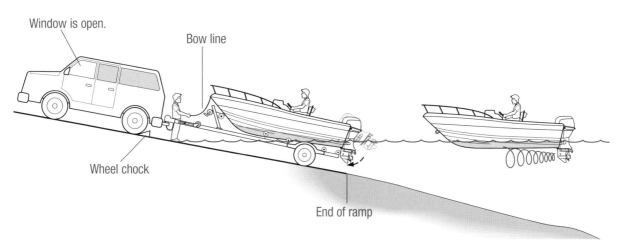

Window is open.

Bow line

Wheel chock

End of ramp

Hauling Out

❶ Back trailer down ramp until about two-thirds of the rollers/bunks are in the water. Park in first or "park" gear and place a chock behind the rear wheel.

❷ Approach trailer slowly, lining up the centerline of the boat with the centerline of the trailer, shift into neutral to let boat float on trailer. Some people prefer to use the engine to get on the trailer, called "power loading," but be aware that some ramp facilities may prohibit this method.

❸ Attach winch cable to boat eye and take up cable until bow is snug against stop. Lock cable. Be sure to operate the winch while standing to one side to avoid getting hit if the cable breaks.

❹ Check that the center of the transom is over centerline of trailer if there are no trailer side posts or guide rails. If the transom is off centerline, try shifting into forward gear at the throttle's "idle" setting and turn outboard to swing transom over centerline. Do not advance throttle.

❺ Raise outboard or stern drive into towing position and lock.

❻ Pull trailer up ramp at slow, steady speed.

❼ Clear the ramp area.

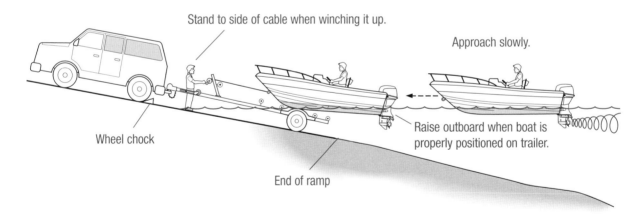

Stand to side of cable when winching it up.

Approach slowly.

Wheel chock

Raise outboard when boat is properly positioned on trailer.

End of ramp

Washing Boat and Trailer

There is an increasing problem with boats and trailers picking up aquatic nuisance species (e.g., zebra mussels) from one body of water and introducing them to other waters or lakes. Away from the ramp and run-off areas, remove the drain plugs and wash down the trailer, boat and boat's gear with high water pressure. Flush the cooling system of outboards with a flusher attachment to the water hose. Remove contents of live wells and bait buckets on land.

Hoist Operation

If a hoist is not operated properly, it can result in serious damage and injury. Some facilities require specific personnel to operate the hoist. If you are not at such a facility and haven't operated the hoist before, ask an experienced person to demonstrate or help. Operate the hoist carefully and don't rush. Often safety rules will be posted. Be sure to review them carefully beforehand.

Hoist Preparation

- Drain any water from the boat and close the drain plugs securely.
- Check the condition of the lifting slings, their fittings, and the attachment points on the boat. Their breaking strength should be at least twice the weight of the boat fully loaded, including fuel and gear.
- Slings are fitted so the boat is level when on the hoist.
- Slings are securely fastened.
- Bow and stern lines are attached to boat.
- Outboard or stern drive is locked in the towing position.

REVIEW QUESTIONS

1. The weight on a hitch ball is known as _____.
2. If the tongue weight is too light, a trailer may swerve back and forth, or _____. If this occurs, _____ speed.
3. When backing a trailer, move the _____ of the wheel in the direction you want the back of the trailer to turn.
4. When launching, once the boat is in the water, park in first gear or "park" and place a _____ behind the vehicle's rear wheel.
5. To avoid introducing nuisance species from one body of water to another, it is important to _____ the trailer, boat and boat's gear after hauling out.

18. Other Boating Activities

KEY CONCEPTS
▶ Personal watercraft
▶ Waterskiing & towed devices
▶ Diving activities
▶ Hunting & fishing
▶ Paddlesports

Personal Watercraft (PWC)

Rear view of the steering nozzle of a PWC.

How Does a Water Jet Work? Personal watercraft are propelled by a water jet drive, which is powered by a gasoline engine located inside an engine compartment. A water jet illustration in Chapter 1 shows how water flows into the jet intake and accelerates through the water pump and squirts out the exit nozzle. It's the jet of water exiting the nozzle that propels the PWC forward. If there is no water coming out of the nozzle, the PWC won't move. When you increase the throttle, water is pumped through the nozzle at a higher speed, resulting in greater thrust that moves the PWC faster. While some models may have a deflector mounted behind the nozzle to deflect or reverse the exiting water, many may not have this feature to stop or reverse the PWC. In this case, you will have to turn off the engine to stop. Make sure you allow enough distance for your watercraft to come to a stop.

Steering. The exit nozzle is movable and is used to steer the PWC. The direction of the nozzle is typically controlled by a handlebar. If you turn the handlebar to the right, it will turn the nozzle to the right causing the thrust from the water jet to turn the PWC to the right. Your steering control improves with the speed of the water exiting the nozzle. Higher engine speeds increase flow and produce greater steering response. If you reduce the throttle to idle or the engine stops, you lose steering control and the amount varies depending on whether your PWC has a device to reduce this loss. In the worse case, the PWC won't change direction even if you turn the handle bar. This occurs because the steering thrust of the jet drive becomes ineffective if the PWC is moving faster than the thrust. A common mistake is to turn while reducing the throttle and then discover you can't change direction.

Maximum capacities label indicating the PWC is limited to 3 persons or 530 pounds (240 kilograms).

Capacity and Stability. PWCs are designed to carry a maximum number of people and/or weight. The recommended capacity can be found in the owner's manual or on the manufacturer's decal. If you exceed these limits, the performance of the PWC could be dangerously affected and could result in capsizing. When operated under the maximum capacities limit with the weight of the occupants centered in the middle, PWCs are stable. When getting on board, keep your weight centered.

If a PWC happens to turn upside down, it should be rolled back upright in the direction recommended by the manufacturer. Failure to do so could result in damage. Check the owner's manual for the direction of rotation and look for a rotation decal on the back (stern) of the PWC.

Fueling. Two key points to remember when fueling:
- fill the tank away from the water, if possible, to avoid polluting the water with fuel spills. Do not overfill your tank.
- gasoline vapor is heavier than air and will sink – after fueling and/or before starting the engine, open the engine compartment and let it ventilate for at least four minutes. If you smell gasoline, check for fuel leaks.

The arrow on this rotation decal indicates the PWC should be rotated clockwise to bring it upright after capsizing.

Starting a PWC. The basic steps are:
1. Complete the pre-start list (includes fuel, oil, required equipment, manufacturer's checks).
2. Position the PWC in an adequate depth of water (as per owner's manual) to avoid ingesting sediment or vegetation into the water jet drive.
3. Get on the PWC.
4. Attach the safety lanyard of the ignition cutoff switch to your wrist or life jacket.
5. Start the engine as per manufacturer's manual.

Falling Off and Re-Boarding a PWC. If you fall off, PWCs typically have an ignition cutoff ("kill") switch that will turn off the engine as soon as you fall off. However, this cutoff switch will only work if its lanyard is attached to the switch and to you. As soon as the lanyard is pulled off the switch, the cutoff switch is activated. Some older models may not have this feature and will circle at idle speed until you can swim over and grab them. Be aware that if the idle speed is set too high, it may be difficult to catch the circling PWC. If you need to re-board the PWC, it should be done from the rear, pulling yourself over the back end and keeping your weight centered.

Equipment and Operating Regulations. PWCs are subject to the same laws, "rules of the road," and equipment requirements that govern boats of the same size. There are additional regulations and requirements specific for PWCs that vary with each state.
- Each person on a PWC must wear a US Coast Guard approved Type I, II, III or V life jacket – a high-impact vest type is recommended.
- Wearing a wetsuit or dry suit is recommended in cool air or water conditions.

Wearing a life jacket is always required when operating or riding on a PWC.

Photo Courtesy of U.S. Coast Guard

• Drivers must attach the safety lanyard to their wrist, or life jacket or clothing (if applicable). If a PWC is equipped with a self-circling device, it must not be disabled.
• Drivers must meet the state's minimum age limit and education requirements.
• PWCs cannot be operated from sunset to sunrise (some states specify one half hour after sunset to one half hour before sunrise, or other variations – check with your state).
• The navigation "rules of the road" apply to PWCs – know them and obey them.
• Obey slow-no wake restrictions.
• Avoid high-speed operation in shallow water, which can cause damage to the water jet pump and environmental erosion.

Boathandling Points

Accident statistics indicate the most common accidents for PWCs are collisions with other vessels or hazards. To help reduce these accidents: keep a proper lookout at all times; stay a proper distance from vessels and objects; and always operate your PWC in a safe manner.

• *Read the operating instructions in the manufacturer's manual and familiarize yourself with stop/start and throttle controls.*
• *Take into account that steering control is drastically reduced or lost when rapidly reducing speed from high to low.*
• *Keep a constant lookout for other boats and objects.*
• *Always look around and behind before turning.*
• *Do not make sudden changes in direction when near other boats.*
• *Do not jump wake close behind another boat (many states prohibit this within 100 feet).*
• *Do not weave through congested traffic.*
• *Be considerate of other boaters and people onshore – avoid operating in the same area for any length of time and avoid making excessive noise (altered mufflers or cutout devices are prohibited in many states).*

Waterskiing

In addition to high-speed boathandling skills, waterskiing and towing wake boards or tubes require additional considerations and skills. States and local jurisdictions may have additional requirements and limitations.

Equipment and Operating Regulations:
• Appropriate USCG approved high-impact life jacket (inflatable type is not suitable) must be worn by a skier.
• Towline: typically 75 feet, but maximum length limitation may vary depending on use and state and local regulations.

- Federal regulations prohibit skiing or towing after sunset and before sunrise; some states have different time limitations – check with your state.
- Have an observer in the boat to watch the skier or towed device, and relay signals to the driver; many states require an observer even if a boat has a rear view mirror.

Driving Tips

- *Use hand signals to communicate.*
- *Wait for a "start" signal from a skier before accelerating and steer straight.*
- *Use a lower speed for inexperienced skiers.*
- *Make wide turns.*
- *Return immediately once a skier falls or drops off.*
- *Make a slow approach when operating near a person in the water – be especially careful with a propeller-driven boat.*
- *Turn off the engine when picking up or dropping off a skier in the water.*
- *Allow a 200-foot wide corridor (or twice the towline length) for the skier to avoid contact with objects.*

Stop

Speed OK

Speed up

Slow down

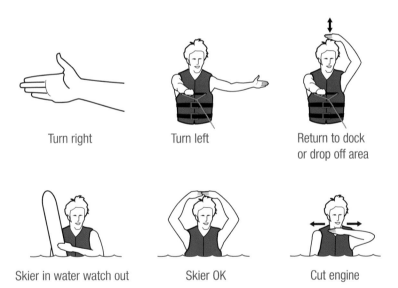

Turn right

Turn left

Return to dock or drop off area

Skier in water watch out

Skier OK

Cut engine

Diving Activities

Under Inland and International Navigation Rules, a vessel engaged in diving operations during the day may display a rigid replica of International Code Flag ALFA not less than 3.3 feet (1 meter) in height. The ALFA flag is exhibited only by a vessel engaged in diving operations and signifies its inability to maneuver in accordance with the Rules. It has no special separation or maneuvering requirements for other boats other than to keep out of the way of the diving vessel.

International Code Flag ALFA (represents the letter, "A")

Sport Divers Flag

The Sport Divers flag has no official status in federal regulations. It is recognized by the Coast Guard as a flag indicating diving operations and, unlike the ALFA flag, it is used to mark locations of divers in the water. Many states have enacted regulations requiring the display of the Sport Divers flag and specify standoff distances. A minimum of 100 feet is recommended but divers frequently stray considerable distances from their marker and separations of up to 300 feet are recommended in open waters. Like the ALFA flag, the Sport Divers flag should be of rigid construction and conspicuously displayed. An operator of a vessel conducting diving operations should only display this flag to mark the site of diving operations.

Hunting & Fishing

If you use your boat to hunt or fish, you should be aware that capsizing and falling overboard account for the greatest number of fatalities (almost 70%) and occur most frequently in boats under 20 feet in length. Eight out of ten fatalities were NOT wearing life jackets. People often hunt or fish in remote areas or during periods of the year (fall, winter or spring) when conditions are cold, weather can change rapidly, and other boaters or marine patrols may not be around if help is needed. You should be aware of the risks of cold water immersion and hypothermia (see Chapter 16). Immersion in cold water is the number 1 killer for people who hunt with a boat.

When you fish or hunt, wear a life jacket. It could save your life.
Photo Courtesy of U.S. Coast Guard

Water Temp.	Wearing Life Jacket	Treading Water	Swimming
70 degrees	18 hours	13 hours	10 hours
55 degrees	3.5 hours	3 hours	2 hours
35 degrees	1.75 hours	1.25 hours	0.75 hours

This table depicts examples of time periods that a person may be able to survive in various water temperatures. (Adapted from U.S. Coast Guard Auxiliary 8th District)

Safety Tips
- *Observe all boating safety rules and regulations. When you hunt or fish, you are a boater and must comply with safe boating practices and regulations.*
- *Wear your life jacket.*
- *Don't overload your boat beyond the limits of the Maximum Capacities label.*
- *Keep the boat evenly balanced.*
- *Keep weights low.*
- *Carry a VHF/DSC radio or cellular phone.*

The best prevention for hypothermia is to dress appropriately in layers, wear a life jacket and a wool or fleece hat, and for cold water wearing a dry suit or wet suit is recommended. Alcohol doesn't mix with boats and cold weather. Not only will alcohol impair your judgment and balance, it will have an adverse effect on the body's ability to avoid hypothermia. Federal regulations require life jackets be carried for each person on board the boat, but if you hunt or fish you should wear your life jacket. If you fall overboard, many boats do not have a good and easy method of getting the person back on the boat and it may take some period of time, especially if you are bulked up with warm clothing that becomes very heavy as soon as you try to emerge from the water. Trying to put a life jacket on in the water is difficult and tiring, and can increase heat loss.

Boat design affects the risk of capsizing and swamping. Many of the smaller boats used for hunting and fishing may have low freeboard (sides), and/or a flat bottom for shallow water operation. Both these features can increase the risk of swamping or capsizing if you overload the boat with people and gear, put too much weight on one side, get caught in rough weather, and anchor from the stern. Boats that have elevated pedestal seats for fishing will have their center of gravity adversely affected when people are sitting in them, which increases the risk of capsizing at smaller angles of heel (tipping).

Paddlesports

Canoeing, kayaking, rafting and rowing are popular watersports, and all use watercraft that are propelled by paddles or oars The easily driven performance of these types of watercraft comes from their light weight and hull shape, but these performance-enhancing features also make them more susceptible to capsizing. With their narrow beam (width) and small amount of draft (depth of hull below the water), they can roll over if the weight of the people and equipment is not kept low and near the centerline. Standing up and shifting your weight to the side can cause capsizing. Avoid reaching too far over the side. If picking up an item in the water, get next to it so your shoulders don't lean over the side. With their low freeboard (height of hull above the water), motor boat wake and rough water conditions could cause these watercraft to capsize or swamp. All boat operators should be particularly careful when operating near these watercraft. Knowing how to swim and wearing a life jacket are smart safety fundamentals. Accident statistics indicate that 50% of canoe and kayak fatalities were while fishing, 25% had consumed alcohol, and a large majority were not wearing life jackets. If you're new to these sports, take a hands-on course. For more information about these courses, contact the American Canoe Association (www.acanet.org) or your state boating department.

Wear a life jacket whenever you canoe or kayak.
Photo Courtesy of U.S. Coast Guard

If you capsize, stay with your craft and try to hold onto your paddle. Hold onto the upstream or upwind end to avoid getting pinned between the hull and a hazard, and float on your back keeping your feet downstream and on the surface to avoid getting them caught in the bottom. Use your free arm to swim to shore.

Safety Tips
- *Wear a properly fitted U.S. Coast Guard approved life jacket.*
- *Know how to swim and paddle.*
- *Know how to self-rescue your craft if it capsizes.*
- *Paddle with a buddy.*
- *Don't paddle or row while under the influence of alcohol.*
- *Be aware of weather and water conditions and forecasts.*

- *Avoid conditions that exceed your skills and experience.*
- *Leave a float plan with a friend or relative.*
- *Wear appropriate clothes, headwear and footwear for air and water temperatures. Wearing bright colors and using brightly colored paddles increases your visibility to other boaters who may not see you low in the water. If in doubt, raise your paddle vertically.*
- *Attach a waterproof bag to carry your personal items: sunscreen, water, VHF/DSC radio or cellular phone, etc.*
- *Check for leaks and carry a bailer.*
- *Don't overload your craft.*
- *Distribute weight evenly, centered side to side and front to back, and keep it low.*
- *Position your weight over the centerline when getting in or out.*
- *Avoid standing up and moving to the side. If you have to move around, keep a secure footing and grip on the watercraft by using the three-points contact method (two hands and one foot in contact or one hand and two feet in contact).*
- *Paddle or row into or away from waves that might capsize or swamp your craft.*
- *Beware of rapids, low-head dams and other hazards along the route.*
- *Paddle near a shore in open waters and avoid channels used by other boats or vessels.*

REVIEW QUESTIONS

1. A jet of water exiting from a moveable _____ is used to steer a PWC.
2. If the throttle is suddenly cut from high speed to idle speed on a PWC, loss of _____ control may occur.
3. When fueling a PWC, you should ventilate the engine compartment for at least _____ minutes before starting the engine.
4. A waterskier is required to wear a Coast Guard approved high-impact _____.
5. If you see a red flag with a white diagonal stripe, it marks the location of _____ and you should keep at least _____ feet from the flag.

Sound Signals & Navigation Lights

Sound Signals

● A short blast is about one second's duration.

— A prolonged blast is from four to six seconds' duration.

For vessels in sight of each other:

● One short blast indicates *altering* course to starboard (International), or *intending* to alter course to starboard (Inland) when meeting or crossing.

●● Two short blasts indicate *altering* course to port (International), or *intending* to alter course to port (Inland) when meeting or crossing.

●●● Three short blasts indicate engine is in reverse (although vessel may still be moving forward).

●●●●● Five short blasts = danger.

For vessels in restricted visibility:

— One prolonged blast every two minutes indicates a vessel under power.

— ●● One prolonged blast followed by two short blasts every two minutes indicates a vessel under sail. Be aware that other vessels will also sound this signal, e.g., vessels engaged in towing, fishing, pushing, and vessels restricted in their ability to maneuver.

Other sound signals:

— One prolonged blast is sounded by a vessel nearing a blind bend of a channel or fairway, or when departing a berth.

For other sound signals consult the *Navigation Rules, International-Inland.*

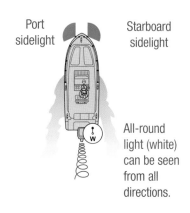

Light requirement for a powerboat underway whose length is less than 39.4 feet (12 meters).

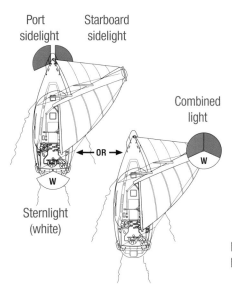

Light requirement for sailboats underway. In addition to sidelights and a sternlight, a sailboat under sail may display a red all-round light over a green all-round at or near the top of the mast, but these lights shall not be exhibited in conjunction with the "combined light" (as shown in the illustration). A sailing boat less than 23 feet (7 meters) long may use a flashlight instead of navigation lights, provided it is turned on in sufficient time to prevent a collision.

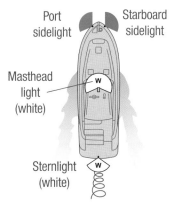

Light requirement for a powerboat (or sailboat using an engine) underway whose length is less than 164 feet (50 meters).

Light requirement for an anchored boat less than 164 feet (50 meters).

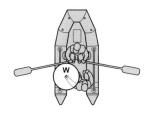

Light requirement for a boat being rowed or paddled: a flashlight is turned on in sufficient time to prevent a collision.

Aids to Navigation Summary

Lateral Aids to Navigation

Lateral marks (below) indicate channels, safe water (mid-channel), and preferred channels (junction buoys) as well as the side on which to leave them when returning from seaward.

Port Side of Channel

GREEN CAN
▶ odd numbered
▶ leave to port

GREEN DAYMARK
▶ odd numbered
▶ leave to port

GREEN BUOY/
GREEN LIGHT
▶ odd numbered
▶ leave to port

PREFERRED CHANNEL
BUOY: GREEN TOPMOST
BAND
▶ preferred channel to
starboard
▶ may have green light
(Fl 2+1)
▶ may be lettered

Starboard Side of Channel

RED NUN
▶ even numbered
▶ leave to starboard

RED DAYMARK
▶ even numbered
▶ leave to starboard

RED BUOY/RED LIGHT
▶ even numbered
▶ leave to starboard

PREFERRED CHANNEL
BUOY: RED TOPMOST
BAND
▶ preferred channel
to port
▶ may have red light
(Fl 2+1)
▶ may be lettered

Middle of Channel

SPHERE/RED & WHITE
VERTICAL STRIPES
▶ safe water
either side

RED & WHITE VERTICAL
DAYMARK
▶ safe water
either side

RED & WHITE VERTICAL
BUOY
▶ sound/light signal
flashes a short and
long white light
(Morse A)
▶ safe water either
side

Isolated Danger and Special Purpose Marks

BLACK & RED BANDS WITH
TOPMARK BUOY
▶ has a topmark of two
black spheres
▶ may have white light
group flashes of two
every 5 seconds
▶ marks an isolated danger
with navigable water all
around

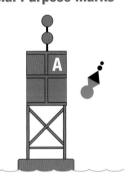

YELLOW BUOY
▶ yellow mark with black
letter(s)
▶ may have a yellow fixed
or flashing light
▶ marks a special feature or
area (e.g., pipelines, traffic
separation schemes, spoil
areas, jetties)

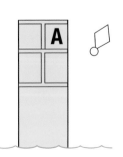

Lighthouses

Lighthouses fall into the category of lighted beacons and are fixed to the sea bottom or on land. Charts indicate a lighthouse with a magenta symbol (looks like an exclamation point) and identify the characteristic flashing sequence of its light (e.g., flashing, occulting, group flashing or isophase). Examples: Fl 15s indicates light flashes once every 15 seconds; Fl(2) 5s indicates a Group Flash 2 every 5 seconds.

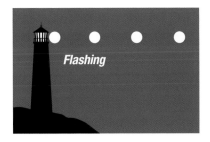
Flashing

Occulting

Group Flashing

Isophase

A **flashing** light is on in short bursts interspersed with longer periods of darkness. A **group flashing** light repeats multiple light signals. A **composite flashing** light repeats irregular multiples of signals, or example "2+1". This means that within its time cycle the light will flash a group of 2 flashes followed by a short pause, then a third flash.

An **occulting** light is on most of the time and "winks" off according to its charted sequence. Sometimes called a "black flash," these lights are easy to take bearings on. An **isophase** light has equal periods of light and darkness.

Information and Regulatory Markers

These markers with their orange symbols and bands are used for dangers, warnings, directions, and other regulatory matters and information.

BOAT EXCLUSION AREA	DANGER	INFORMATION	CONTROLLED AREA

Explanation may be placed outside the crossed diamond shape, such as dam, rapids, swim area, etc.	The nature of danger may be indicated inside the diamond shape, such as rock, wreck, shoal, dam, etc.	Directions, distances and other non-regulatory information is displayed inside the square or rectangular symbol.	Type of control is indicated in the circle, such as slow, no wake, speed limit, etc.

Glossary of Boating Terms

*including radio phonetic alphabet
(in parentheses)*

A (Alfa)

Abeam - off the side of (at right angle to) a boat.

Aboard - on a boat.

Adrift - a boat drifting without control.

Aft - at or toward the stern or behind a boat.

Aground - a boat whose bottom, keel or skeg is touching the sea bottom.

Alternator - a device which generates electricity from an engine.

Amidships - toward the center of a boat.

Astern - behind the stern of a boat.

Athwartships - across a boat from side to side.

B (Bravo)

Back - a counterclockwise change of wind direction.

Bail - to empty a boat of water.

Barometer - a weather forecasting instrument that measures air pressure.

Battery switch - the main electrical cutoff switch.

Beam - the width of a boat at its widest point.

Bear away - to fall off, turn away from the wind.

Bearing - the direction from one object to another expressed in compass degrees.

Below - the area of a boat beneath the deck.

Berth - 1. the space in which you park your boat. 2. a bed on a boat.

Bight - a loop in a line.

Bilge - the lowest part of a boat's interior, where water will collect.

Bimini - a sun awning used to cover the cockpit or flying bridge.

Bitter end - the end of a line.

Block - a pulley on a boat.

Boat hook - a pole with a hook on the end used for grabbing hold of a mooring or retrieving something that has fallen overboard.

Bottom - 1. the underside of a boat. 2. the land under the water.

Bow - the forward part of a boat.

Bow line (BOW - line) - a line running from the bow of a boat to the dock or mooring.

Bowline (BOE-lin) - a knot designed to make a loop that will not slip and can be easily untied.

Breast line - a short dockline running perpendicular from the beam (at mid-length) of a boat to the dock.

Broach - a sudden, uncontrolled and powerful turn when running down a large wave. The boat will also roll on its side and in extreme situations could capsize.

Bulkhead - a wall that runs athwartships on a boat, usually providing structural support to the hull.

Bunk - see berth, definition #2

Buoy - a floating mooring ball or navigation mark.

Buoyancy - the ability of an object to float.

C (Charlie)

Cabin - the interior of a boat.

Can - an odd-numbered, green buoy marking the left side of a channel as you return from seaward.

Capsize - to turn a boat over on its side or upside down and not return to its upright position.

Cast off - to release a line when leaving a dock or mooring.

Cavitation - vaporized bubbles disrupt water flow on the propeller blades causing loss of thrust and erosion of the blades' surface.

Centerline - the midline of a boat running from bow to stern.

Chafe - wear on a line caused by rubbing.

Channel - a waterway where the water is deeper than the surrounding area and is often marked by navigation marks.

Chart - a nautical map.

Chart plotter - an electronic device used to display charts and determine positions, bearings, distances and courses.

Chine - the sharp edge formed at the intersection of the topsides and bottom of a boat.

Chock - a guide mounted on the deck through which docklines and anchor lines are run.

Choke - a device for controlling the mixture of air and fuel for an engine.

Cleat - a nautical fitting that is used to secure a line.

Coaming - the low protective wall surrounding the cockpit.

Coastal waters - include the U.S. waters of the Great Lakes, U.S. territorial seas and those waters directly connected to the Great Lakes and territorial seas where any entrance exceeds 2 nautical miles between opposite shorelines to the first point where the largest distance between shorelines narrows to 2 miles.

Cockpit - the area that is recessed below the deck or gunwale in which seats and boat controls are located.

Coil - to loop a line neatly so it can be stored.

Companionway - the steps leading from the cockpit or deck to the cabin below.

Compass - the magnetic instrument that indicates the direction in which a boat is headed.

Compass protractor - a plotting instrument oriented to latitude-longitude lines on a chart.

Compass rose - the twin circles on a chart which indicate the direction of True North and Magnetic North.

Console - a structure in a cockpit or inside a boat on which the boat controls and instruments are located.

Contour line - a line of constant water depth on a chart.

Course - the direction in which a boat is steered.

Course Over Ground (COG) - a boat's course over the surface of the planet.

Crew - anyone on board who helps the operator (person in command) with handling the boat.

Crosscurrent - the direction that is perpendicular (at 90 degrees) to the direction of the horizontal movement of water.

Cross-track error (XTE) - the distance and direction that a boat is off course (off track) to the activated waypoint.

Crosswind - when the wind direction is perpendicular (at 90 degrees) to a boat's course or its centerline.

Current - the horizontal movement of water caused by tides, wind and other forces.

D (Delta)

Datum - a standard vertical reference from which tide depths are calculated, or a standard geographic coordinate system (latitude & longitude) of the earth's surface from which the position of a boat or object can be determined.

Dead reckoning (DR) - used to determine a boat's position calculated from course steered and speed (distance) through the water.

Deck - the mostly flat surface area on top of a boat.

Deck plate - a circular plate installed at openings in a deck and fitted with a threaded watertight cap if connected to fill lines for fuel or water tanks or pumpout lines for holding tanks.

Deviation - is the magnetic compass error caused by iron or steel objects with magnetic properties.

Diameter (propeller) - the dimension of the circle made by the rotation of the tip ends of the propeller blades.

Dinghy - a small boat that can be rowed or sailed.

Displacement - the weight of a boat; therefore the amount of water it displaces.

Dividers - an instrument used for measuring distances or coordinates on a chart.

Dock - 1. a structure to which a boat can be tied. 2. the act of bringing a boat to rest alongside the structure.

Dockline - a line used to secure a boat to a dock.

Dodger - a canvas shield in front of the cockpit of some boats that is designed to protect people from spray.

Downcurrent - see downstream.

Downstream - in the same direction that the horizontal movement of water is flowing toward.

Downwind - away from the direction of the wind.

Draft - the vertical distance from the water's surface to the deepest point on a boat.

E (Echo)

Ease - to let out a line.

Ebb - an outgoing tide.

EPIRB - Emergency Position Indicating Radio Beacon

F (Foxtrot)

Fairway - the center of a channel.

Fall off - see head down.

Fast - secured.

Fathom - a measurement of the depth of water. One fathom equals six feet.

Fender - a flexible cylindrical or spherical object used to protect the sides of a boat when coming in contact with a dock or another boat.

Fitting - a piece of nautical hardware.

Fix - a boat's position determined by bearings.

Flake - to lay out a line on deck using large loops to keep it from becoming tangled.

Flood - an incoming tide.

Float plan - an itinerary of your intended trip, left with a responsible party onshore.

Float switch - a switch for an electric bilge pump that is activated when water raises a floatable lever to a certain level.

Following sea - waves hitting the boat from astern.

Fore - forward.

Forepeak - a storage area in the bow (below the deck).

Forward - toward the bow.

Fouled - tangled.

Freeboard - the height of a hull above the water's surface.

G (Golf)

Gear - generic term for boating equipment.

Gearshift - the control that changes the direction of an engine and its propulsion system (propeller or jet drive) from neutral to forward or reverse.

Give-way vessel - the vessel required to give way to another vessel when they may be on a collision course.

Great Lakes - means the Great Lakes and their connecting and tributary waters including the Calumet River as far as the Thomas J. O'Brien Lock and Controlling Works (between mile 326 and 327), the Chicago River as far as the east side of the Ashland Avenue Bridge (between mile 321 and 322), and the Saint Lawrence River as far east as the lower exit of Saint Lambert Lock.

Ground tackle - the anchor and rode (chain and line).

Gunwale (GUNN-nle) - the top edge of the topsides.

Gust - an increase in wind speed for a short duration.

H (Hotel)

Hard over - to turn the tiller or wheel as far as possible in one direction.

Hatch - a large covered opening in a deck or the top of a cabin.

Haul in - to tighten a line.

Head - the bathroom or marine toilet on a boat.

Heading - the direction of the boat expressed in compass degrees.

Head down - to change course away from the wind.

Head off - see head down.

Head up - to change course toward the wind.

Headway - progress made in the forward direction.

Heave - to throw.

Heavy weather - strong winds and large waves.

Heel - the sideways lean of a boat caused by torque from the propeller, side force from the rudder (when turning) or wind.

Helm - the tiller or wheel.

Helmsman - the person who drives a boat.

Holding ground - the sea bottom used to hold a anchor.

Holding tank - a tank that collects sewage from a marine toilet (head).

Hull - the envelope of a boat formed from a number of surfaces such as bottom, topsides, transom, cockpit, deck, and cabin.

Hull speed - the theoretical maximum speed of a boat determined by the length of its waterline.

I (India)

Inboard - inside of the rail of a boat.

Inverter – a device that converts DC (direct current) battery power into AC (alternating current) electricity.

J (Juliet)

Jury rig - an improvised, temporary repair.

K (Kilo)

Kedge off - to use an anchor to pull a boat into deeper water after it has run aground.

Keel - a vertical fin running along the centerline of a powerboat's bottom to improve its tracking ability by reducing its sideways slip in the water.

Kill switch - a switch that shuts off the engine and is activated by the release of an end of a cord from a button or an ignition switch.

King spoke - a marker on the steering wheel which indicates when the rudder is centered.

Knot - one nautical mile per hour.

L (Lima)

Land breeze - a wind that blows from land toward the sea.

Lash - to tie down.

Latitude - on a nautical chart, the geographic distance measured north or south from the equator in units of degrees, minutes, decimals of minutes or seconds.

Lazarette - a storage compartment accessed through the deck, usually located in the stern.

Lee shore - the shore to which the wind is blowing.

Leeward (LEW-erd) - the direction away from the wind (where the wind is blowing to).

Leeward side - the side of a boat that is away from the wind.

Leeway - sideways slippage of a boat in a direction away from the wind.

Left-hand (propeller) - a propeller that rotates counterclockwise in forward gear when viewed from astern (behind).

Lifeline - plastic coated wire, supported by stanchions, around the outside of a deck to help prevent people from falling overboard.

Lifesling - a floating collar, which doubles as a hoisting sling, is attached to the boat by a length of floating line and is used to retrieve a victim from the water.

Line - a nautical rope.

List - the sideways lean of a boat caused by more weight (i.e., people, equipment, fuel) on one side.

Longitude - on a nautical chart, the geographic distance measured east or west of a line running from the north pole through the Greenwich Observatory in England to the south pole in units of degrees, minutes, decimals of minutes or seconds.

Lubber's line - a small post in a compass used to help determine a course or a bearing.

Lull - a decrease in wind speed for a short duration.

M (Mike)

Magnetic - in reference to Magnetic North rather than True North.

Marlinspike - a pointed tool used to loosen knots.

Master switch - see battery switch.

Mayday call - the internationally recognized distress signal for a life-threatening emergency.

Mooring - a permanently anchored buoy to which a boat can be tied.

Marine Sanitation Device (MSD) - a marine toilet system that treats or stores the effluent to meet the requirements of the Clean Water Act.

N (November)

Nautical mile - a distance of 6076 feet, equaling one minute of the earth's latitude.

Navigation aids - include beacons and buoys as well as lighted ones that are used to determine a boat's position or safe course, or to warn of dangers or obstructions.

Navigation lights - lights (i.e., sidelights, sternlight, masthead light, etc.) that are used to identify watercraft and help avoid collisions when operating from sunset to sunrise and during restricted visibility.

Navigation plan - includes compass headings, distances and estimated times to help you determine your boat's position or find your way during your intended trip.

Navigation Rules - laws established to prevent collisions on the water.

No-discharge zone - an area where the discharge of any treated and untreated sewage is prohibited.

Nun - a red, even-numbered buoy, marking the right side of a channel as you return from seaward. Nuns are often paired with cans.

O (Oscar)

Offshore - away from or out of sight of land.

Offshore wind - a wind that blows from land toward the sea.

Onshore wind - a wind that blows from the sea onto land.

Outboard - outside the rail of a boat.

Overtaking - a boat that is catching up to another boat and about to pass it.

P (Papa)

Painter - the line attached to the bow of a dinghy.

Pan-Pan call - the internationally recognized distress signal for an urgent situation.

Parallel rulers - an instrument with two rulers linked parallel by hinges used to plot a course.

Pendant - see pennant.

Pay out - to ease a line.

Pennant - a length of line used to attach a boat to a mooring.

Personal Flotation Device (PFD) - a life jacket or vest, life ring or other U.S. Coast Guard approved flotation device.

Piling - vertical timber or log driven into the sea bottom to support docks and/or secure docklines.

Pitch (propeller) - the theoretical distance that a propeller would advance in one revolution in a solid material (no slippage).

Plot - applying calculations to a chart to determine course or position.

Port - 1. the left side of a boat when facing forward. 2. a harbor. 3. a window in a cabin on a boat.

Power-driven vessel - any vessel propelled by machinery.

Power trim - hydraulic adjustment of the angle of outboard motors or stern drives while underway.

Prevailing wind - typical or consistent wind conditions.

Prop walk - the side force generated from the rotation of a propeller, which results in a boat's tendency to turn slightly instead of tracking straight.

Propeller - a hub with radiating blades used for propulsion.

Pulpit - a stainless steel guardrail at the bow and stern of some boats.

Pumpout station - a location where boats can empty their holding tanks.

Q (Quebec)

Quarter - the sides of the boat near the stern.

Quarter berth - a bunk located under the cockpit.

R (Romeo)

Radar reflector - a metal object designed to be detected by other vessels' radar.

Rail - the outer edges of a deck.

Range - the alignment of two objects that can be used to indicate a channel or safe water or stay on course.

Raw-water - the water in which a boat floats.

Restricted visibility - any condition in which visibility is restricted by fog, mist, falling snow, heavy rainstorms, sandstorms, or any other similar causes.

Rhumb line - a straight course between two points.

Right-hand (propeller) - a propeller that rotates clockwise in forward gear when viewed from astern (behind).

Rode - line and chain attached to the anchor.

Route - on either a GPS or chart plotter, a series of pre-planned waypoints that define a trip.

Rudder - the underwater moveable fin used to steer a boat.

Running lights - see navigation lights.

S (Sierra)

Safety harness - strong webbing worn around the chest and attached to the boat to prevent a person from being separated from the boat.

Sailing vessel - any vessel under sail provided that propelling machinery, if fitted, is not being used.

Scope - the ratio of the amount of anchor rode deployed to the distance from the bow to the bottom.

Scupper - a cockpit or deck drain.

Sea breeze - a thermal generated wind that blows from the sea onto land.

Seacock - a through-hull fitting with a valve.

Seaplane - any aircraft designed to maneuver on the water.

Secure - make safe or tie a line to a cleat.

Sécurite call - an internationally recognized signal to warn others of a dangerous situation.

Set - 1. the direction of a current. 2. to dig an anchor into the sea bottom.

Shackle - a metal fitting to connect lines, wire, chain and other fittings.

Shoal - shallow water that may be dangerous.

Skeg - 1. a triangular fin on the centerline at the aft end of a powerboat's bottom to improve its steering and tracking ability. 2. a triangular fin at the bottom of the lower unit of an outboard motor.

Skipper - an informal term for a person in charge of a boat.

Slip - 1. see berth #1. 2. to cast off from a mooring using a doubled line.

Snub - to hold a line under tension by wrapping it on a winch or cleat.

Sole - the floor in a cockpit or cabin.

Solenoid switch - an electrical switch which shuts off the flow of propane.

Soundings - water depths on a chart.

Speed Over Ground (SOG) - a boat's speed over the surface of the planet.

Spring line - a dockline running forward or aft from a boat to a dock to keep the boat from moving forward or aft when used in combination with bow and stern lines, or to swing a boat when powering against it.

Squall - a short intense storm with little warning.

Stanchion - a stainless steel support at the edge of a deck which holds the lifelines.

Stand-on vessel - the vessel required to maintain its course and speed when it may be on a collision course with another vessel (unless the give-way vessel does not take action to avoid a collision).

Starboard - when looking from the stern toward the bow, the right side of a boat.

Steerage - ability to control direction of a boat when steering with a wheel or tiller.

Steerageway - minimum amount of boat speed needed to control its direction with a rudder.

Stem - the centerline or structural member on the forward profile of a hull running along the profile from the deck to approximately the waterline.

Stern - the aft part of a boat.

Stow - to store properly.

Sump - 1. a low point in the bilge where water from rain or leaks collect. 2. a tank where drain water from showers and iceboxes collect.

Swamped - filled with water.

T (Tango)

Tackle - a sequence of blocks and line that provides a mechanical advantage.

Throttle - a device for controlling the engine's revolutions per minute (rpm).

Tide - the rise and fall of water level due to the gravitational pull of the sun and moon.

Tiller - an arm used to steer a boat instead of a steering wheel.

Toe rail - a low rail around the outer edges of a deck.

Topsides - the sides of a boat between the waterline and the deck.

Track - a course a boat has run or will follow if it stays on its heading.

Transom - the vertical surface of the stern.

Trim - 1. the relationship of a boat's forward and aft orientation to the water's surface, i.e., level trim (same as designed orientation), bow up or down trim, stern up or down trim. 2. to adjust the angle of outboard motors or stern drives, i.e., to trim up or down.

U (Uniform)

Underway - means that a vessel is not at anchor, or made fast to the shore, or aground.

Upstream - the direction that is opposite to the direction of the horizontal movement of water.

Upwind - toward the direction of the wind.

V (Victor)

Variation - the angular difference between Magnetic North and geographic (True) North in units of degrees and minutes.

Vee-berth - a bunk in the bow of a boat that narrows as it goes forward.

Veer - a clockwise change of wind direction.

Velocity Made Good (VMG) - the speed a boat has made toward its destination.

Ventilation (propeller) - air from above is drawn onto the propeller blades disrupting water flow over the blades that causes a sudden loss of thrust and increase in engine rpm.

Vessel - includes every description of watercraft, including non-displacement craft, WIG craft and seaplanes, used or capable of being used as a means of transportation on water.

Vessel engaged in fishing - any vessel fishing with nets, lines, trawls, or other fishing apparatus which restricts maneuverability, but does not include a vessel fishing with trolling lines or other fishing apparatus which do not no restrict maneuverability.

VHF - abbreviation for Very High Frequency, a two-way radio commonly used for boating.

Visibility - *Vessels shall be deemed to be in sight of one another* - only when one can be observed visually from the other.

W (Whiskey)

Wake - waves caused by a boat moving through the water.

Waterline - the horizontal line on the hull of a boat where the water surface should be.

Waypoint - a point or location used in navigation and identified by its latitude and longitude.

Western Rivers - means the Mississippi River, its tributaries, South Pass, and Southwest Pass, to the navigational demarcation lines dividing the high seas from harbors, rivers, and other inland waters of the United States, and the Port Allen-Morgan City Alternate Route, and that part of the Atchafalaya River above its junction with the Port Allen-Morgan City Alternate Route including the Old River and the Red River.

White caps - waves with foam tops.

Windage - the amount of surface area of a boat that is presented to the wind.

Windlass - a type of winch used for handling anchor rodes (line and chain).

Windward - the direction toward the wind (where the wind is blowing from).

Windward side - the side of a boat closest to the wind.

X (X-Ray)

Y (Yankee)

Index

Acknowledgements

A number of US POWERBOATING/US SAILING powerboat instructors and trainers, and other experts, were involved in reviewing and editing this revised edition of *Start Powerboating Right!* which was originally written by Dick Allsopp and Timothea Larr. They include: Dick Allsopp, Charlotte Arms-Cartee, Joe Brandt, Steve Colgate, Rob Crafa, Mark Ellis, David Forbes, Mike Huffer, Brian Kfoury, Timothea Larr, Karen Prioleau, Doug Sparks, Lynn Walls and Kate Williams. Their suggestions and edits were included for the most part, but on a few occasions compromises were made.

The new material on electronic navigation was written by Tom Cunliffe and incorporated into the previous edition's navigation chapter which had been based on his *Coastal Navigation* book written for the United States Sailing Association. There are more than 40 new illustrations drawn by Joe Comeau who was the original principal illustrator of this book, and Diane Cacase has continued her role as production design manager in charge of layouts and design.

The U.S. Coast Guard's Boating Safety Division is a primary source for much of the material in Chapter 10.

Photography credits include: Dick Allsopp, Boston Whaler, Inc., Cummins MerCruiser Diesel Zeus (ZF Marine), Tom Cunliffe (chart plotter screens), EdgeWater Powerboats, Groco, Rosamond Larr, Timothea Larr, Anne Martin, Medeiros Boat Works, The Moorings®, Moran Towing, Ralph Naranjo, NOAA, Raritan Engineering, Mark Smith, Standard Horizon, Teleflex Marine, Thetford Corp., and U.S. Coast Guard.